Citizen-Centered Cities, Volume I

Citizen-Centered Cities, Volume I

Case Studies of Public Involvement

Paul R. Messinger

With contributions from Marco Adria, Fiona Cavanagh, Michelle Chalifoux, Moein Khanlari, Edd LeSage, Heather Stewart, and Rosslynn Zulla

 BUSINESS EXPERT PRESS

Citizen-Centered Cities, Volume I: Case Studies of Public Involvement
Copyright © Business Expert Press, LLC, 2017.

First published in 2017 by
Business Expert Press, LLC
222 East 46th Street, New York, NY 10017
www.businessexpertpress.com

ISBN-13: 978-1-60649-658-9 (paperback)
ISBN-13: 978-1-60649-659-6 (e-book)

Business Expert Press Service Systems and Innovations in Business and Society Collection

Collection ISSN: 2326-2664 (print)
Collection ISSN: 2326-2699 (electronic)

Cover and interior design by S4Carlisle Publishing Services
Private Ltd., Chennai, India

First edition: 2017

10 9 8 7 6 5 4 3 2 1

Printed in the United States of America.

Dedication

Dedicated to my aunt,
Susan Frances Messinger—
a dedicated Chicago city planner.

Abstract

This casebook was inspired by a commissioned systemwide review of the public-engagement activities of the Transportation Services Department of the City of Edmonton. These cases cover a wide range of public-involvement projects:

- neighborhood street modifications to reduce accidents,
- a controversial "signature" bridge,
- doubling of the light rail transit system,
- a new highway interchange,
- routine road repairs that trigger demands for retail-friendly street planning,
- bicycle routes that cannibalize car lanes,
- plans for goods movement (freight) to facilitate industry and economic growth,
- guidelines for multiuse urban streetscaping, and
- a transportation master plan into which all of the above fits.

All these projects involve the transportation system—the backbone of a city—common to municipal planning worldwide. The cases are animated by an electorate of digitally connected citizens who eschew surprises, expect inclusion, and demand balanced decision making. This casebook addresses the question: how do city administrators function in this new reality?

These cases facilitate discussion about several perplexing issues. Is stopping a plan at citizens' behest a success? What happens when "a unique piece of urban architecture" removes a century-old landmark and traverses native burial grounds? If the public is excluded from decision making, is it sufficient to collect representative viewpoints beforehand and choose the best plan on technical grounds? What happens when the "hangtime" between concept consultation and passing of a budget for a massive light rail plan is nearly 40 years? How should cities use stakeholder input groups? What happens if transportation planners are ahead of where citizens in terms of their "green" orientation? How can industry be integrated with residential life? How can principles of urban design and streetscaping be encouraged? How much public engagement is enough? Why is it critical to "close the loop" with citizens to let them know the impact on decision making of their input.

This casebook opens with a chapter that takes a comprehensive look at nine challenges for public involvement in modern cities. Many aspirational recommendations are provided for each challenge. The cases benefit from close access to city participants and documents: depth interviews, a detailed survey of participants, and review of city documents, consultant reports, public media coverage, practitioner articles, and academic literature. Overall, this casebook provides a body of experience in digestible form that would take years for a municipal administrator to accumulate on the job.

Keywords

city management, collaborative governance, municipal service delivery, municipal transportation services, participatory democracy, public consultation, public involvement, service systems

Contents

Foreword

The work in this casebook began as a systemwide review of the public-involvement activities of a department of the City of Edmonton. The Transportation Services Department employed about 3,000 people working in all aspects of planning, operations, and public consultation for transportation for the city. The goal of the systemwide review was to assess the department's public-involvement activities from the perspective of the department, after reviewing data from multiple sources. I served as principal investigator; the rest of the team initially consisted of Fiona Cavanagh, who at the time was Director of the Centre for Public Involvement; Marco Adria, who was Academic Director of the Centre; and Edd LeSage, emeritus professor and founding director of a related research unit, the City Region Studies Centre at the University of Alberta. We hired three graduate students at the University of Alberta (selected from many applicants) to help with the data collection and analysis: Moein Khanlari, a PhD candidate who I was supervising at the School of Business with specialization in marketing, who served as facilitator and chair of research meetings; Heather Stewart, a masters student from political science; and Rosslynn Zulla, a PhD candidate in the School of Public Health. Our contact in the City's Transportation Services Department was Michelle Chalifoux, who served as part of the research team, providing reports, access to city managers, and constructive critiques of intermediate conclusions.

The progress of our project was reviewed periodically by an advisory committee, consisting of Greg Heaton, City of Edmonton, Sustainable Development; Stephane Labonne, City of Edmonton, Community Services; Cory Segin, City of Edmonton, Office of Public Engagement; Noreen Rude, City of Calgary, Office of Public Engagement; Mac Logan, City of Calgary, General Manager of Transportation; Dr. Julia Abelson, McMaster University; Jill Bradford-Green, City of Edmonton, Former Manager of Public Involvement; Councilor Ben Henderson, Edmonton City Council; and Elaine Solez, Edmonton Federation of Community Leagues. Originally, the data collection was planned to be limited to interviews with key department managers and a survey with city employees involved with public consultation, as well as a review of the practitioner and academic literature. Evaluative materials from citizens of Edmonton were intended by the city to be collected as part of a separate project. Early in the research, the advisory committee suggested that we consider particular cases of public involvement in Edmonton as part of the basis for review. The material gathered for these cases provided in-depth background for the team's report to the city, which was submitted in 2015, and reviewed by City Council that summer. It turned out that the actual case material was too lengthy to include in the report to the city. These cases, after elaboration, synthesis and polishing, constitute the bulk of the present volume. In the course of the project, we wondered how Edmonton compared with other cities, and I suggested covering the largest cities of Canada and a similar number of representative cities in the United States. The resulting twelve short city studies of public involvement constitute the bulk of a companion volume.

Chapter 1 of the current volume consists of a distillation of the themes developed in a report provided to the City of Edmonton, leaving out specific assessments of and material only relevant to Edmonton. I wrote the first draft of the report in the form of a series of challenges, followed by discussion in the context of Transportation Services in the City of Edmonton, and a series of recommendations. The writing and organization of these challenges was edited by Marco Adria. Michelle Chalifoux provided refinements, informed by her experience in the City of Edmonton, to support the key themes of the report. Fiona Cavanagh extensively added to the number of detailed recommendations, reflecting her inclination to commit to paper her experiences with public involvement as Director of the Centre for Public Involvement. It was then suggested by the advisory committee that the recommendations be grouped as short term, long term, those only relevant to transportation, and those applicable for the larger city corporation. In view of their large number, the recommendations were intended to be aspirational. The City immediately implemented several of the recommendations; and it is hoped that more implementation will follow. Only those recommendations that are potentially applicable for other cities are included in Chapter 1. The number and extent of these recommendations cuts a broad swath—a selection potentially useful for consideration by administrators in most cities.

The cases that follow contain a rich compendium of the workings of public consultation. As Santayana noted, "those who cannot remember the past are condemned to repeat it"; but this is far too harsh an assessment for the City of Edmonton, because the cases document successes, inevitable frustrations, and evidence of learning.

The cases for Edmonton focus on transportation projects; and one thing that is common across all cities is the centrality of the transportation network—the backbone of a modern city. The conclusions, nevertheless, appear to carry over to public involvement in other activities, including planning for and operation of public buildings, recreation centers, parks, neighborhood renewal, museums, and public art. Transportation is also critical to ongoing operations of police, fire, real estate, and other municipal services. The planning for a bridge, which falls under transportation, has much in common with the architectural planning of a public building and the selection of a large piece of public art, for example.

Candidate topics for the Edmonton cases were suggested by Michelle Chalifoux, and selected with the help of the advisory committee. I wrote the Twin Brooks and Burnewood Area case, and recommended a unified organizational structure for all the Edmonton cases to include sections on (1) Context and Catalyst, (2) Planning, (3) Engagement, (4) Impact, (5) Assessment and Learning. The cases open with a paragraph or two containing a statement of the key problem or issue (possibly also including a photo or illustration); the cases end with sources (and possibly an appendix). I worked closely with the student researchers assessing information as it was gathered, suggesting directions, and writing and rewriting sections. The opinions in the cases reflect a consensus reached between the student researcher and me. Sincere thanks are due to the City of Edmonton for open access to information about these cases. Reflecting their roles, the student researchers are listed as first authors for their respective cases.

The cases from Edmonton cover a range of experiences:

- The Twin Brooks and Burnewood Area case demonstrates that withdrawing a plan can be a success if consultation indicates that the community does not want the changes in the first place.

- The Walterdale Bridge case provides an architype of copious information gathering prior to decision-making and vigorous dissemination of possible plans (and even selection from these), but with little involvement of the public in the decision-making that occurred in between. The case asks the question: if the planners and city council ultimately made the best decision, should things have been done differently?

- The Valley Line Expansion case involved even higher stakes (investment of $1.8 billion, essentially doubling the light-rail transit system in Edmonton) and unprecedented "hangtime" (nearly 40 years between conception, first communication with stakeholders, and final drawing up of plans). Nevertheless, recent progress has been fairly smooth, with a masterful, somewhat lucky, social media push to bring the provincial government along as a funding partner.

- Unlike the previous cases, the Interchange at 149th and Yellowhead Trail case proceeded routinely and effectively from the onset, starting with public involvement integrated with concept planning and also using stakeholder input groups effectively.

- The 99th Streetscape represented a missed opportunity when larger-than-usual street maintenance raised the expectations of an active community organization in an area buzzing with evening life and community spirit. By the time the community called for more concerted streetscape planning—and the city was ready to agree—ongoing construction was already contracted for and too far along to change in the current cycle.

- The Bicycle Routes case, in contrast, shows the city getting ahead of what the neighborhood residents and businesses wanted. This case shows that getting too far ahead of citizen expectations can be as problematic as being too far behind them.

- The Compete Streets case subsequently shows the city developing a general policy to avoid some of the issues that arose in the previous two cases (99th Streetscape and Bicycle Routes). A Complete Street includes a desired level of diversity in user types and transportation modes accommodating safe and efficient movement of cyclists, pedestrians, transit users, motorists, buses, and some delivery trucks.

- Unlike all the above cases which targeted citizen residents and local retail and other businesses, the Goods Movement case, required engaging industry and many other stakeholders to optimize flow of goods movement essential to the local economy.
- Lastly, the Transportation Master Plan comes back full circle with a description of early public engagement. All the previous cases build on this master plan.

This casebook closes with suggested readings. The most directly relevant past academic and practitioner work is contained in the set of readings at the end listed as "Readings in Public Involvement." These were gathered mostly by the student research assistants and other student's I have directed in master's programs. Those readings with more than 100 Citations in Google Scholar, as of July 2016, are marked as "* highly cited"; those with more than 500 Citations are marked as "** very highly cited." With time, the exact number of citations can only increase, but the relative standing may remain generally accurate. The reading by Rowe and Frewer (2000) is among the most highly sighted in this group, and, more recently, I find Bryson et al. (2012) provide a useful synthesis. The book by Grunig (1992) is foundational and also among the most widely read and used. A second set of "Readings on e-Government and Participatory Government" is provided. This is based on readings collected by student teams in a class I taught on city government. I find that Bonsón, et al. (2012) and Mossberger, et al. (2013) provide, respectively, interesting comparative description of countries' e-government activities in Europe and states' e-government activities in the United States. Finally, a set of readings on service, e-service, self-service, and disruptive technologies is included to provide background from the service and business literatures. Among the many highly cited works, particularly influential have been the framework on service-dominant logic by Vargo and Lusch (2004) and the earlier Gap Model by Parasuraman, Zeithaml, and Berry (1985).

As a whole, this casebook provides a body of experience in digestible form that would probably take years for a municipal administrator to accumulate on the job. The hope is that cities will benefit from this range of experience.

Paul R. Messinger

Acknowledgments

A debt of gratitude is owed the City of Edmonton, Department of Transportation Services, for access to reports, to key managers for interviews, and to departmental personnel for a survey (121 professionals responded from 311 contacted), for invaluable guidance from Michelle Chalifoux, Public Engagement Program Manager, and for grant support to hire three graduate students researchers. Appreciation is also expressed to the University of Alberta for support to draft a Partnership Grant Letter; to the Kule Institute for Advanced Study for support for a new undergraduate class on municipal service delivery; to IBM for research support about Smart Cities, to the Town of Devon, Alberta for support for a study on "Leveraging Online Engagement in Rural Municipalities," and to Walmart for Seed Grant funding. Many thanks are due to the thoughtful suggestions of a capable advisory committee, consisting of Greg Heaton, Edmonton Sustainable Development; Stephane Labonne, Edmonton Community Services; Cory Segin, Edmonton Office of Public Engagement; Noreen Rude, Calgary Office of Public Engagement; Mac Logan, Calgary General Manager of Transportation; Dr. Julia Abelson, McMaster University; Jill Bradford-Green, Former Edmonton Manager of Public Involvement; Councilor Ben Henderson, Edmonton City Council; and Elaine Solez, Edmonton Federation of Community Leagues. Lastly, the spirited suggestions of Susan Francis Messinger, Chicago City Planner are gratefully acknowledged.

PART 1

Challenges and Opportunities for Putting Citizens First

CHAPTER 1

Nine Challenges for Public Involvement 2.0

Paul R. Messinger, Marco Adria, Edd LeSage, Fiona Cavanagh, Moein Khanlari, Heather Stewart, Rosslynn Zulla, Michelle Chalifoux

Service delivery increasingly involves users co-creating value with a service provider. Users co-create value by doing many activities as self-service. Users also cooperate in service design by offering suggestions on what is needed and providing feedback about prototypes and new service offerings. New services have leveraged the Internet, mobile, and other new technologies to facilitate co-creation of value only a few clicks away. This book focuses on how cities are increasingly incorporating co-creation of value with citizens in municipal service delivery. For municipalities and other democratic governments, a major component of co-creation of value consists of "public involvement."

Public involvement is an evolving concept in an emerging field. Related terminology with similar connotations in this area includes *public engagement, collaborative governance, civic renewal, participatory democracy, and citizen-centered change.* These terms have shades of difference in meaning, based on the degree of action implied for citizens. Public involvement is the broadest category of activities in this domain. We define *public involvement* as inviting, encouraging, and using contributions from citizens about important issues that affect them, in ways that lead to better decisions and improved democratic outcomes.

Cities are increasingly carrying out public involvement, particularly in North and South America and Europe, facilitated by new technology. But despite the best of intentions, it has proved difficult for cities to do public involvement. Several factors in the current environment relevant to successful rollout of public involvement are the following:

- To involve citizens in decision-making meaningfully, cities require a healthy, vibrant culture, along with widely supported political and social practices. Cities in North America are facing rapidly shifting demographics and complex problems, including infrastructure development, that require thoughtful, informed responses by citizens.
- Online public involvement has not yielded the positive results for which its promoters had hoped. Online participants can suffer from groupthink or seek influence out of proportion to their numbers. Methods of combining online information and interaction with face-to-face processes are necessary.
- Public involvement is an antecedent of civic renewal, but it is not a substitute for concrete change. Citizens and their governments must be prepared to follow up meaningful public-involvement processes with an action agenda.

In spite of these factors, the positive outcomes and benefits of public involvement are substantial and well documented. The research literature identifies at least six expected benefits of high-quality and comprehensive public-involvement practice, summarized in Table 1.1.

Further benefits of public involvement include the following: (a) Effective public involvement has the potential to build trust within society. (b) Online public involvement can attract individuals and groups who otherwise would not participate in civic matters. (c) Cities can attract the interest of young people at institutions of higher education, in particular, who may be more likely to make those cities their home after graduation. (d) Enhanced information systems can facilitate systematic and routine incorporation of citizen learning and preferences into

Table 1.1 Six expected benefits of public involvement

Legitimacy: Decisions that account for public values balance "fact-based" or "expert" decisions, and add legitimacy and depth to decisions.

Better decision-making: Drawing on the diverse experiential knowledge of the public informs decisions that can then be made based on real needs.

Reduced polarization: Well-structured processes, with intentional opportunities for dialogue and deliberation, save time and resources by seeking "common ground" and by constructively uncovering and utilizing conflict. This increases "public-minded" decision-making and responses to policy problems.

Improved capacity: Citizens acquire skills and competencies for listening, problem solving, and creative thinking.

Engaged citizens: Citizens develop a civic sense of purpose in their lives as they devote energy and time to shaping public policy.

Inclusiveness: Mechanisms are created to take advantage of the diversity of the population by reducing barriers to participation, especially for minority and underrepresented groups.

decision-making. (e) Cities can draw on innovative methods and the civic history of other municipalities.

Building on this last point, this casebook is designed to help cities learn from each other about experiences with public involvement. These cases illustrate standard difficulties that municipalities encounter when carrying out public involvement. For convenience of data collection, the nine cases come from Edmonton, Alberta, Canada (a metropolitan area of about one million people), and the cases deal with transportation services in one form or another. On the basis of extensive communications with city professionals from other cities, including Calgary, Vancouver, and Chicago, the problems identified in these cases appear to be common in many cities; so the learning from these cases is not restricted to one medium-sized city in western Canada. (Moreover, to provide broader depth across cities, in a companion volume, we also provide twelve overview descriptions of public involvement as it is carried out in six U.S. cities and six Canadian cities.)

In this chapter, we introduce the topic by summarizing nine broad challenges for cities to achieving excellence in the practice of public involvement. Each challenge is followed by various recommendations. The recommendations collectively point toward an evolved approach to public involvement.

Conceptual Framework for Assessing Municipal Public Involvement

Although not required for understanding the challenges and recommendations below, a conceptual framework was used to guide the development of our analysis of public-involvement practices. The framework represents a service orientation to understanding public involvement. It consists of the three major components of service: Commitment, Conduct, and Outcomes.

This framework breaks public-involvement processes into Planning, Engagement, Impact, and Assessment/organizational learning. Conduct (or practice) is preceded by Commitment and followed by Outcomes. Several criteria for excellent public involvement emerge from Figure 1.1: (1) Planning, (2) Engagement, (3) Impact, (4) Assessment, (5) Buy-In, (6) Support, and (7) Outcomes. The Outcomes can be further subdivided into Quality Projects, Involved Citizens, and Perceptions of Usefulness. These criteria can be used as the basis for developing a "report card" for a municipality's public involvement. Such an assessment of a city's public involvement can be done through consideration of interview data or through surveys.

Nine Challenges for Public Involvement and Associated Recommendations

We propose that many cities today face nine challenges for carrying out effective public involvement, summarized in Table 1.2.

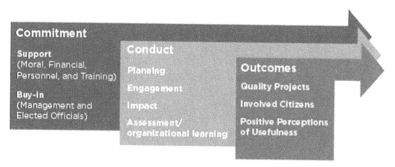

Figure 1.1 Our framework for public involvement

Table 1.2 Nine challenges for public involvement in city management

1. In pursuing excellence in public involvement, cities are facing rising citizen expectations.
2. Cities are increasingly expected to employ a transparent and predictable budgeting process for public involvement, but in some instances are not funded to do so.
3. Cities are struggling to combine excellence in engineering and planning with excellence in public involvement.
4. A culture of learning and innovation in the practice of public involvement has yet to be fully developed in many municipalities.
5. Cities are falling behind in their capacity to evaluate their public-involvement initiatives.
6. In public-involvement initiatives, municipalities are contending with the management problems of decision lock-in, hang time, participant churn, and misaligned expectations.
7. In public-involvement initiatives, cities are not always able to acquire a balance and range of public perspectives.
8. Municipalities are finding that the public-involvement spectrum, while useful, requires selective and strategic use.
9. Closing the information loop with citizens is emerging as a significant gap in public-involvement practice in municipalities.

We identified these nine challenges through the process of writing the cases in this casebook and the city studies in a companion casebook. We also relied on three additional sources of information: (1) interviews with administrators and professional staff in the Transportation Services Department of Edmonton, Canada, (2) a survey from 121 professionals involved with carrying out public-involvement activities in Transportation Services in Edmonton Canada (a 38.9 percent response rate from 311 professionals contacted who were judged to do public-involvement activities in Transportation Services), and (3) a review of city reports, articles in public media, literature combining practice-based and professionally oriented publications, and scholarly publications about public involvement generally and for public-transportation work specifically.

In this chapter, we do not attempt to "prove" that these nine challenges hold in all cities. Detailed documentation indicating the presence of these challenges in Edmonton, Canada, is provided elsewhere (Review of Public Engagement 2015, City of Edmonton, Department of Transportation Services, by the same author team). On the basis of our discussions with professionals working in several large and small municipalities in Canada and the United States, we believe that several of these challenges are applicable elsewhere. To some extent, assessing such empirical claims is tedious and very detailed—like what some say about visiting a sausage factory: "many of us like the product, few of us want to see it being made." We leave it to readers to judge the extent to which these nine generalizations hold in their own municipalities.

For each of these challenges, in this chapter we provide several recommendations, more or less closely tied with the challenge itself. These recommendations are aspirational—in the sense that it is not realistic to expect a municipality to implement a large number of these recommendations at once. These recommendations are provided for generating ideas and discussion, to help organizations begin to identify the lowest hanging fruit first. Additional policies can be added according to what seems to work. We suspect that the larger the city, the more explicit the planning efforts have to be because there is greater danger of a "disconnect" between those making the decisions and those affected by them.

The recommendations in this chapter are designed to encourage the embedding of public involvement into the organizational design of a city and its departments. The central goals of our recommendations, each tied with one of the nine challenges, are summarized in Table 1.3.

The recommendations associated with Challenges 1 through 5 concern the development of an organizational culture that takes into account a clear strategy of public involvement. The recommendations associated with challenges 6 through 9 concern institutionalized processes for planning and carrying out public-involvement activities and for making use of citizen contributions.

Movement toward what we might call "Public Involvement 2.0" will require attention to some of the items in Table 1.3. It will require a well-developed learning plan for staff and increased development of key skills and competencies. To support this movement, evaluation criteria will need to be established, with the goal of creating a culture of best practices in which learning about public involvement is shared, recognized, and rewarded. Such an effort also requires effective use of information

Table 1.3 Steps toward building Public-Involvement Capacity

Development of Organizational Culture
1. Unify the approach to communication about public involvement, both with the public and within the organization.
2. Increase the budget for public involvement and clarify the budgeting process.
3. Signal organizational commitment to public involvement by explicitly referring to public-involvement priorities, skills, and outcomes in job descriptions, consulting contracts, and staff-recognition programs.
4. Foster learning opportunities, a system-wide learning plan, and a learning culture.
5. Measure and reward excellence in public involvement.
Ongoing Planning and Administrative Policies
6. Create policies and procedures for continuity of public involvement for projects with long lifecycles.
7. Achieve a balance and range of perspectives on issues for which public-involvement initiatives are designed.
8. Encourage the use of more active forms of public involvement (on the public-involvement spectrum).
9. "Close the loop" with citizens about how their contributions were used in policy and decision-making.

and communications technologies, including information systems and social media, for both internal and external audiences.

We now outline nine key challenges that municipalities face with public involvement. Following the statement and discussion of each of the nine challenges, a list of detailed recommendations is offered, more or less directly tied to the challenges. The first elements of the list are short-term recommendations, and the second, are long-term recommendations. We provide a general discussion (brief if possible) associated with each of these challenges and sets of recommendations.

In what follows, it should be noted that we use cities and municipalities interchangeably (although we recognize that these may be of very different sizes, of course). Furthermore, many of the quotes we cite are from interviews with engineers in Transportation Services in Edmonton. Nevertheless, we expect that similar views about public-involvement activities would come from city planners and managers of specialized operations in other branches of a municipal administration in other municipalities, and we have found casual confirmation of this expectation.

Challenge 1: Rising Expectations for Public Involvement

In pursuing excellence in public involvement, cities are facing rising citizen expectations.

> *The central problem in most democracies is . . . that citizen expectations and capacities have undergone a sea change in the past 20 years, and our public institutions have not yet adjusted to the shift.*
>
> —Matt Leighninger,
> Author and Public-Involvement Practitioner

Over the past two decades, there has been an increasing demand for public access to the planning and decision-making processes of governments and public agencies. This has been a consequence of many social changes, but among these are increasing access to information through the Internet and the rise of "expert citizens" who have a higher level of education and who have at their disposal more effective modes of communication. Scholars and practitioners argue that new approaches to public involvement will require a commitment to two-way communication between citizens and the municipality, to shared authority, and to facilitating communication among citizens and municipalities listening to this communication.

Elected representatives, administrators, and staff are commonly skeptical about the capacity of citizens to inform planning. Conversely, many citizens are skeptical about the ability of public institutions to understand and respond meaningfully to citizen contributions. New methods, structures, technologies, tools, and networks can be used to bridge this gap between expectations for change on the one hand and caution on the other. A starting point to meeting rising expectations is through communications (see Table 1.4).

Challenge 2: Budgeting Process for Public Involvement

Cities are increasingly expected to employ a transparent and predictable budgeting process for public involvement, but in some instances are not funded to do so.

Table 1.4 Recommendations for Challenge 1:

"In pursuing excellence in public involvement, cities are facing rising citizen expectations"

1. **Develop a public online portal or web page from which citizens can easily find up-to-date information about key city policies and projects.** This resource should include information about the public-involvement activities that were associated with such projects. It could also be used to engage citizens for contributing to future projects.

2. **Establish a visual communications initiative.** Initiate some pilot work on selected projects in which visual and graphic design students, marketing students, and adult educators collaborate with engineers to implement some creative and innovative ways to share complex, technical information with citizens and stakeholders. See the Centre for Urban Pedagogy, in New York for examples of making policy accessible.

3. **Communicate success indicators in public involvement, learning opportunities, and ways to participate.**

4. **Establish a public-involvement citizens' board.** The Board would advise and support a municipality in various desired focal areas as it oversees its public-involvement program. Members of the Board should be selected so as to reflect the municipality's demographics and diversity of opinion. The case of Portland, with an advisory committee comprised of both City staff and citizens (the PIAC, or Public Involvement Advisory Council), provides useful insights and resources for exploring this possibility https://www.portlandoregon.gov/oni/48951. The City of Montreal has also piloted the use of borough-level citizen advisory councils.

Long-term Excellence in Public Involvement

a. **Develop and communicate a charter of roles, rights, and responsibilities for planning.** This recommendation could be accomplished by, for example, establishing a "3 Rs" policy applying to rezoning and planning decisions, defining the roles, rights, and responsibilities for all participants. The charter could provide a guide for "rules of involvement"—a set of expectations for listening, information sharing, decision-making, providing feedback, debating, and collaborating (adapted from City of Vancouver Task Force).

b. **Establish an annual large-scale city-wide deliberative process for citizens on the top issue of the year, using both face-to-face and online involvement tools.** The top issue might be practical, focusing on implementation, such as routing new bike lanes, or it could be broader and more values based, such as developing principles for establishing the City's annual budget.

Life is not just a series of calculations and a sum total of statistics, it's about experience, it's about participation, it is something more complex and more interesting than what is obvious.

—Daniel Liebeskind, Architect

Cities must ensure adequate resourcing for public involvement and must balance funding across competing demands and priorities. These demands come from community groups and citizens, and from administrators and elected representatives. We now turn the rationale for our specific recommendations shown in Table 1.5.

Edmonton, for example, with a large public-involvement commitment, budgets less than 0.1 percent of the transportation services budget (CA$488.7 million in 2013) for explicit public-involvement-related activities. Nevertheless, department staff members work on public-involvement activities throughout the year without earmarked budgets for this. From our surveys, we found that 40 percent of respondents were spending more than 10 percent of their time on public involvement, and 12 percent were spending more than 25 percent on public involvement. A senior engineer stated, "if you were to go back let's say even a decade,. . . the City typically didn't do a lot of what I'd call a large scale public involvement. It was more project-based." This has changed dramatically, and considerable effort is now devoted to public-involvement activities on a continual basis, with new responsibilities given to employees without specific budgets for public involvement. Other interviewees emphasized the need for dedicated funding for public involvement and allocation of staff time for public-involvement activities. Funding is also required for media services in order to inform citizens about public-involvement activities. Contracting is required for specialized training for moderators and facilitators for public involvement. Respondents also noted that, in recent years, fewer specialists have been employed, and staff has taken on duties previously contracted out. According to one manager, the public-involvement budget for capital projects can range from 1 percent to 20 percent of the project cost, depending on the perceived need and complexity. At the same time, when asked how adequate the resources allocated for public involvement were, almost half (46.3 percent) of staff respondents believed that resources for public involvement were "good" (34.7 percent) or "excellent" (11.6)—the others indicated "fair" (25.6 percent), "weak" (10.7 percent), "Inadequate" (3.3 percent), or "Not Sure" (14 percent). In this context, overall, it may be desirable for transportation planners to make the budgeting process for public involvement more explicit and perhaps larger. One way to assure attention to and skill at public involvement is to hire more professionals who specialize in and support public-involvement activities across a range of projects.

Table 1.5 Recommendations for Challenge 2:

"Cities are increasingly expected to employ a transparent and predictable budgeting process for public involvement, but in some instances are not funded to do so"
1. **Budget explicitly for public involvement and increase the amounts dedicated to it.** This can be accomplished over time as priorities for public involvement are identified and resource implications become clearer.
2. **Dedicate a cadre of staff who will specialize and support public involvement throughout the organization.** Staff specialists can be dedicated to managing public-involvement projects and to training other staff, developing a community of practice (COP) within the municipality, developing leaders in the area, and improving evaluation policies and practices.
Long-term Excellence in Public Involvement
a. **Develop a public-involvement process for reviewing new capital projects.** Such a review would be the first step in the project's potential for stimulating new roles for citizens in shaping the project.

An open issue concerns quantifying the benefit generated from public involvement. One interviewee commented, "I think what would be really useful is to get. . .a sense of the value of the time spent in public involvement, in terms of. . .the feedback we get from citizens. What's the value in using that information to help in a positive way influence our decisions and outcomes?" Such a quantification of value does not exist at the moment, and is difficult to get. However, we argue that publishing performance indicators for the public should be the first step toward eventually allowing the City of Edmonton, at a corporate-wide level, to quantify the value of public involvement. This could be done by considering the benefits of public involvement that have been identified in the literature: increased legitimacy for decisions, better decision-making processes, reduced conflict, improved citizen capacity, and a strengthened culture of citizen involvement.

Challenge 3: Attaining Excellence in Public Involvement

Cities are struggling to combine excellence in engineering, planning, and operations with excellence in public involvement.

We are what we repeatedly do. Excellence, then, is not an act, but a habit.

—Aristotle

The nature of the mandate of many municipal departments requires a large proportion of specialized professionals (including engineers, planners, operations managers of law enforcement, and so on) and technical and administrative staff who support the work of these groups. For these groups, added to the earlier core measures of success (e.g., efficient and effective management of operations, attending to budgets, meeting deadlines, ensuring safety, achieving high-quality design and construction) is an additional core measure of success—that of excellence in public involvement. (See Table 1.6 on page 17 for specific recommendations.)

Emphasizing public involvement can take time and cost money, and hence may be seen to stand at odds with existing core measures of success. At the very least, public involvement can be seen to require additional planning and funding that is not available or that might be diverted from existing project funds. As one of our interview respondents noted, "some don't see the value or return on investment of spending money on public involvement; public involvement takes money from the project." Other considerations that limit or detract from the creation of a culture of public involvement are as follows: (1) failure to integrate the allocation of time and resources to expert technical requirements on the one hand and public-involvement requirements on the other; (2) uneven attempts to coordinate technical considerations in a project with the contributions made by citizens during the public-involvement process; (3) low levels of funds provided for public-involvement training, professional development, and capacity building for expert technical and administrative staff; and (4) lack of effort to recognize individuals and teams for excellence in public involvement.

The basic tension between the tradition of excellence in engineering, planning, or operations, and the new emphasis on excellence in public involvement is also reflected in a divergence in opinions about whether it is easy to incorporate citizen contributions into project decisions. Approximately 41 percent of our survey participants disagreed with the statement, "in our projects, it is difficult to incorporate public input," and about 34 percent agreed with the statement (25 percent were neutral). An interview respondent stated,

> We have to balance the public involvement and feedback with con-flicting themes. There's no way we're ever going to make everybody happy. I would give more weight to the technical considerations and the dollars because we're responsible ultimately to the City as a whole. I would lean more towards giving a little bit [of] favour to the technical considerations and a little less favour to the public.

The tension between public involvement and technical considerations to which this respondent refers, and the means by which it is usually re-solved, may be increased by a lack of clarity of the role that elected repre-sentatives play in identifying priorities. Another tension to be considered is between the emerging value of public involvement in public organiza-tions and the "guild" values of professional engineering in a department like Transportation Services. Sanctions exist within the profession, and more broadly in law, for deviating from practice standards. From the pro-fessional's perspective, care must be taken before adopting the advice or opinions of "lay" citizens. Efforts to rebalance engineering expertise and the value of public involvement may be restrained by requirements to ad-dress professional standards and even the risk of professional culpability in departing from established standards.

Interview respondents expressed the positive impacts of public in-volvement, but they also stated that integrating citizen contributions into the decision-making process for a Transportation Services project is dif-ficult. They stated that proposals by citizens may not be technically safe. Similarly, they stated that such proposals may not be relevant to the par-ticular stage of the project lifecycle or the subjects being discussed. There may be little or no time or budget to implement such proposals. One interview respondent compared the values of engineers and of citizens, who for the respondent were represented or typified by planners:

> [E]ngineers are the same. We defend our designs, they defend their urban plans. It's a different skill set and a different mind-set. So again, I'm not saying that you couldn't have a planner or couldn't have an engineer, but you have to have that mindset that you want to actually capture what the public concerns are and

deal with that as opposed to try to attach yourself to any particular design or any particular plan. I brought through a couple of engineers who worked here for five or six months, and they said I can't do this because you put them in public meetings and they just don't do well, period. You have to have a different attitude and a different mindset when you're out there in the public, and very good engineers. If you don't like doing that, if you don't like being in the public, and you don't like having to sit there and explain and consider other options the public might bring up, you're going to have a real tough time being part of the program.

The significance of such problems was weighted differently by interview respondents. For example, one interview respondent suggested that having a public-involvement professional associated with a project made the difference. In terms of the time required to capture, assess, and use citizen contributions, the respondent stated:

> The one thing that I find the hardest on the plans that we're working on internally is actually documenting and analyzing the feedback that we get. Because it takes a fair bit of time. You get all of these survey forms, whether they're electronic or hardcopy, and then you have to do something with them and ultimately summarize them and figure out what to do in terms of balancing that with the technical aspect. So oftentimes having a public-involvement person helps a lot because they can digest that information and come up with some of the key themes. It's more of a summary for us that then helps to ease up on our workload.

In summary, some respondents cited the problems, tensions, and difficulties of public involvement as evidence that public involvement often provided only limited benefits for a project. If public involvement was of value, according to this argument, it was not for engineering purposes. On the other hand, other interview respondents argued that citizen contributions can beneficially and directly inform design considerations, although not always. Acquiring high-quality contributions from citizens depends to some extent on the public-involvement competence of staff.

Table 1.6 Recommendations for Challenge 3:

"Cities are struggling to combine excellence in engineering, planning, and operations with excellence in public involvement"
1. **Review and update job descriptions and ensure that duties in public involvement are assessed as a part of performance.** Such duties should include the requirement to document and share learning about the effectiveness of public involvement.
2. **Develop new public-involvement standards that are specific to the context of the relevant municipal departments.** These standards would seek a level of excellence in relation to public involvement in complex technical areas and the communication of technical problems and topics to citizens. Such standards would be shared across city departments and could be the basis for dissemination and collaboration activities with professional groups such as the International Association for Public Participation (IAP2).
3. **Ensure that citizens and city staff have distinct roles and expertise in the public-involvement process.** This could be done through developing a guide or visual for use during public-involvement events. It could also be done by providing different examples to staff about the kind of contributions that citizens are in the best position to provide. Examples might include community-specific or geographic-specific knowledge, expression of citizen values, and statements of priorities and preferences.
4. **Review the roles and responsibilities of external contractors.** Find a balance between using external public-involvement expertise and building internal skills, knowledge, and capacity.
Long-term Excellence in Public Involvement
a. **With a relevant municipal department, establish an award of excellence in public involvement for engineers or students.** See an example from New Zealand: http://nzeeawards.org.nz/2014/Forms/ NZEEA_EntryJudgingCriteria_Community-Engagement-2014.pdf. The award could be the basis for developing a set of best practices for public involvement in engineering. A roundtable session featuring the work of award winners could be held as part of a developing community of practice (COP).
b. **Add corporate-wide evaluation of public involvement to the mandate of a particular department.** Performance indicators will be the key to developing a common understanding between the municipality and citizens as to how well public involvement is being carried out. The department would have a corporate-wide mandate that would enable it to carry the evaluation function as a permanent part of its portfolio.

Challenge 4: Building a Culture of Learning about Public Involvement

A culture of learning and innovation in the practice of public involvement has yet to be fully developed in many municipalities.

Management is about arranging and telling. Leadership is about nurturing and enhancing.

—Tom Peters, Management Consultant and Author

Achieving excellence in public involvement requires departmental commitment and leadership (see Table 1.7). Public involvement is a rapidly evolving field in which core ideas and practices are revisited, adapted, and refined. Learning and innovation in public involvement are required to ensure that staff members are contributing to the level of excellence.

Respondents to our survey collectively recognize their personal knowledge and skills in public involvement is midway between "fair" and "good" (Mean = 3.60/5), below the nominal standard of "good" (4.0/5). And only 41 percent of survey respondents stated that they have benefited from professional development or training opportunities in public involvement.

An interview respondent commented on the task of moderating discussion tables at an open house:

> We had a plan and there were a lot of internal meetings to devise a strategy around how we were going to facilitate those processes and who would lead. And we separated out the 12 to 15 citizens at different tables, and we all took responsibility for facilitating discussions at tables. We had a couple of techs at one and then an engineer at another, and we shared the burden and load. But for the most part it was done by sink or swim. We threw people into these experiences. I mean there was no formal training. [We had to] learn on the fly.

To respond to such expressions of need, informal and semistructured learning opportunities are of great importance for organizational learning. They allow workgroups and individual staff to learn from the successes and challenges of others. Besides such learning opportunities, it is desirable to have manuals, guidelines, and other tools available for use in designing and carrying out public-involvement initiatives. (Such tool exist in the City of Edmonton, however, staff in Transportation Services appeared to be largely unaware of the existence of these tools.) In rapidly developing areas of knowledge and practice, collegial sharing is often at the center of organizational learning. Such collegial sharing can also occur across departments or in meetings with professionals from other municipalities. Learning is an important part of an effort to improve and sustain excellence in public involvement.

Table 1.7 *Recommendations for Challenge 4:*

"A culture of learning and innovation in the practice of public involvement has yet to be fully developed in many municipalities"

1. **Create a public-involvement learning plan.** The plan should identify the key skills needed by staff and should make reference to the internal and external opportunities for learning. The plan should have a budget and other resources for organizational learning. Create an innovation fund that staff can apply to use for testing and piloting new or adapted public-involvement methods.

2. **Offer leadership training to project managers to support excellence in public involvement.** This could be accomplished through a leadership module or short course to examine the changing nature of public administration in a context of rising citizen expectations. The emphasis would be on fostering new skills, developing planning processes, and supporting a long-term vision for public involvement.

3. **Develop a campaign designed to educate and train staff in the principles and practices of excellent public involvement.** Part of the campaign could include creating incentives for recognizing excellent public involvement.

4. **Ensure that staff members are available in the organization to promote skill development, best practices, and innovation.**

5. **Establish a COP, with the purpose of collegially sharing experience and knowledge in public involvement.** The COP should possess adequate expert, administrative, and budget resources. Create online and physical archive tools to allow the COP, and workgroups, to retain, share, and learn from successes and challenges of others. Ensure that participation in the COP is included in job descriptions and assessed in performance evaluations.

6. **Offer learning opportunities to citizens.** Learning resources, tools, modules, and short courses for citizens and community groups could be created to allow for a deeper public understanding and knowledge of municipal planning process and the contextual factors and challenges that influence communities. Learning opportunities for citizens would also provide new opportunities for staff to exchange views with communities.

7. **Support training in public involvement for engineering students.** Establish collaboration between the city and local universities and colleges. The purpose would be to encourage engineering education to include principles and practices for public involvement.

8. **Create a digital engagement strategy and plan for communications and engagement projects.** Create organizational ties to enable the use of open data and data analytics.

Long-term Excellence in Public Involvement

a. **Increase civic literacy and civic education through such methods as citizen academies.** The goal for the learning would be to encourage citizens to understand the complexities, challenges and opportunities of involvement of decision-making in relation to key community issues. Outcomes of the learning would be high-quality feedback from citizens in subsequent public-involvement activities.

b. **Create reporting tools and templates for sharing knowledge corporate-wide.** A first step might be to encourage development of case studies within the municipality following the format of the cases in this book. Information from managers could be compiled in an online survey about the completed public-involvement project entered into a database and printed out in a case-study format.

Special attention should also be paid to aggregating and transferring practice-generated knowledge, experiences, and best practices. Many organizations have benefited by establishing a community of practice (COP), championed by management and established with formal supports and sustained through the interest and energy of staff. A formal COP is well suited to the area of public involvement, given the burgeoning nature of the field in which a great deal of useable knowledge has not been formalized.

Challenge 5: Evaluating Public Involvement

Cities are falling behind in their capacity to evaluate their public-involvement initiatives.

Quality is never an accident. It is always the result of intelligent effort.

—John Ruskin

Evaluation is critical to the success of public involvement in the long run (for specific recommendations see Table 1.8). Evaluation can contribute to incremental progress in quality improvement of practices. Constructive evaluation also builds public trust in the public-involvement process by demonstrating a strong commitment to learning, improvement, and excellence. However, assessing the effectiveness of public-involvement efforts is not commonly undertaken in practice in a systematic fashion, as a scholar in the area notes in an examination of public-involvement practices in public organizations in the United States:

> At present, there exist no systematic comparisons of citizen participation processes and methods, despite the fact that agency officials are increasingly required to engage the public.

> (Nabatchi 2012, icma.org/Documents/Document/Document/ 303516).

The lack of attention to evaluation follows from the multidimensionality of public involvement as a concept. Evaluation relies on a clear determination of what quality means and how it should be measured. In

Table 1.8 Recommendations for Challenge 5:

"Cities are falling behind in their capacity to evaluate their public-involvement initiatives"
1. **Create a multi-year public-involvement evaluation and performance-measurement framework.** Include narratives of the history and assessment of public-involvement processes.
2. **Determine key public-involvement success indicators, identify procedures for choosing success criteria in consultation with citizens, and choose appropriate data-collection methods.** While some success indicators can be considered as standard elements for all public-involvement projects, others can be chosen through consultation with citizens.
3. **Ask staff and contractors to report on how citizen contributions from public-involvement activities were used, why, and why not.** Templates can be developed to standardize these feedback mechanisms across projects.
4. **Communicate success indicators in public involvement.** These would be included and reported on a city online Citizen/City Dashboard.
5. **Create metrics for demonstrating to citizens the likelihood that citizen contributions will influence decision-making and to what extent.** Present such metrics at the beginning and end of public-involvement initiatives.
Long-term Excellence in Public Involvement
a. **Implement an annual report card on public involvement.** Convene citizens, community groups, staff and administrators, and elected representatives to establish corporate-wide indicators of excellence and an evaluation framework. Results would be reported on an online Dashboard.
b. **Establish a corporate-wide award for individuals and workgroups for their accomplishments in public involvement.**
c. **Host a corporate-wide annual meeting on evaluation methods and results from the preceding year.** Such a meeting would contribute to cross-departmental sharing of expertise.

addition, public involvement tends to take in many stakeholders with varying interests and concerns, and the context for each public-involvement initiative differs significantly.

A large set of criteria exists for measuring the two overarching dimensions of the *fairness* of public-involvement processes and the *competence* associated with the design and execution of public-involvement projects. These measures are often categorized into process and outcome criteria. *Process* criteria include representativeness, transparency or perceived openness, process flexibility, independence, resource accessibility, task definition, structured decision-making, early involvement, cost-effectiveness, convenience, and satisfaction. *Outcome* criteria include influence on decisions and policies, impact on public trust, and staff and public awareness of and attitudes toward public-involvement practices. (For further background, see Rowe & Frewer 2000, "Public participation methods: A framework for evaluation." *Science, technology & human values* 25, 1: 3-29). Of course, data collection for measuring such criteria must be planned at the early stages of a public-involvement project.

A related issue for city professionals is ascertaining how much public involvement is enough to meet a professional standard.

> When do we and when can we say independently outside of the expectations of City Council that we have effectively engaged the majority of the public? To me that's another big question that we really need to talk about, because there's a perspective out there that you may have done better. But you still haven't quite done good enough, you haven't quite got to enough people, or you haven't really represented the people you should've engaged.

If public involvement is a new professional standard that municipal employees must meet, it is only fair to let experts trained in other fields know in quantitative terms what the standard is. This sentiment is evident in the case study about the Twin Brooks and Burnewood Area Projects.

Challenge 6: Decision Lock-in, Hang Time, Participant Churn, and Misaligned Expectations

In its public-involvement initiatives, municipalities are contending with the management problems of decision lock-in, hang time, participant churn, and misaligned expectations.

> *Good management is the art of making problems so interesting and their solutions so constructive that everyone wants to get to work and deal with them.*
> —Paul Hawken, Environmentalist and Author

The problems we identify in this challenge arise out of the long lifecycles of major city projects. Such projects include construction of roads, interchanges, and light rail transit (LRT); landscaping and construction within parks; building of recreation facilities; and even planning of entire

Figure 1.2 Stages in the lifecycle of a major project

new neighborhoods. Design and construction of such projects can extend over many years. The long lifecycle creates distinctive management problems associated with the effective practice of public involvement. Before considering these problems in detail, we want to first describe their interrelations, by way of the stages of the project lifecycle.

Figure 1.2 describes the project lifecycle as depicted in standard planning form by the City of Edmonton. This particular graphic, with a particular stage highlighted, is used consistently in city documents, for internal communications and for communications with the public, to indicate how far along a project is. The lifecycle has five stages, forming together what is referred to as the "Project Stage Indicator Framework." For a given project, public-involvement activities may be carried out at one or more of the five stages. However, most public involvement occurs at the Concept and Design stages.

Problems with managing public involvement arise from variations in how and when the stages of the project proceed. For example, the five stages of a project may vary in length of time, with one project having a long period of time devoted to the Strategy and Concept stages while another devotes a longer period of time to the Design stage. In addition, the stages are not always distinct, with the Build stage beginning before Design is complete. There can be gaps of time between stages, sometimes extending for several years. These variations in the length and progression of the stages are "normal business" for departments, such as Transportation Services or City Planning, because projects in these departments are by their nature complex, dependent on changing technologies and economic conditions, and subject to shifts in political decision-making. For the management of public-involvement activities, four main problems arise, which we discuss in turn (recommendations follow in Table 1.9, pages 28-29).

Decision Lock-In. Citizens who join a public-involvement initiative at one of the later stages in the project lifecycle may want to revisit decisions made at an earlier stage. Citizens who have become active in public involvement at the Design stage, for example, may want to reconsider the decisions already made in the Concept stage. When this happens, the problem of decision lock-in arises. Citizens who join the public-involvement process can become disillusioned because they feel their contributions have not been considered. They may seek to undermine or bypass public-involvement initiatives. Public distrust and even hostility may become evident. Such an outcome arose in some cases in this book, such as the Walterdale Bridge case study (p. 53).

Interview respondents suggested that it is important to continually assess the perspectives of key individuals and groups and ensure their commitment throughout the duration of a project. They also stated that it would be desirable to have a single staff member, possessing skills and knowledge of the technical aspects of a project as well as community consensus building, to manage the public-involvement process from Strategy to Operation. Regardless of staffing arrangements, interviewee respondents stated that management of public involvement must extend to the end of the project. It must provide citizens with feedback on how their contributions have been incorporated into final decisions. This last conclusion is evident in the case study about the Twin Brooks and Burnewood Area Projects (p. 47).

The certainty that stems from decision lock-in is necessary for project progress; but it also reduces the flexibility for changes along the way. After preliminary engineering and concept approval, a large portion of a budget for a capital project is set. Establishment of the budget to build a capital project provides a level of certainty that the project will be realized in some form. The scope of public involvement necessarily changes as a project moves forward and decisions are taken, but citizens consulted later in the process often want to revisit decisions already taken. As one manager noted:

> [For] bigger scale projects, where we're actually building new roadways or widening, for example, we'll hold an Open House on [a plan that is] 60% to 100% completed . . . to let the public know, and once again see if they have any major comments, which we mostly likely won't follow.

At this stage, the general project is already understood to be a "go," the budget is locked-in, and the main design elements are complete. The same manager noted that with rehabilitation projects, funds are typically limited, "also we can't add anything extra . . . that the public's asking for."

The scope of public consultation usually becomes more circumscribed as the successive project stages are completed. For example, after the Design stage, the purpose of public involvement will be to inform citizens about the broad directions of the project, although citizens may be invited to provide feedback about particular design elements, such as aesthetic choices for LRT stations, streetscape improvements, and landscaping.

Hang Time. The entire lifecycle of a Transportation Services project may span just six months. In this case, changing perceptions, shifting economic conditions, and fading memories may present no problem. In other cases, a project lifecycle may span more than 30 years, as in the case study on the Valley Line Expansion (p. 65). For that project, the Strategy and Concept stages took place in the mid-1970s, followed by an extended hiatus, after which the Design stage, complete with budget, was approved in 2014. The extremely long lifecycle stages—that is, hang time—create at least three difficulties.

The first difficulty is motivating citizens to provide input early in the project lifecycle, during the Strategy and Concept stages. Foundational changes in the project are possible during these stages, but many citizens cannot see the value of their participation when the outcome is many years out. An interview respondent in the Department describes a conversational scenario between staff and a citizen:

> The first question asked is, "Are we building this?" "No." "Oh, well, then I'm not interested. When are you going to build it?" "Well, maybe 15 to 20 years." "I'll be moved by that time, so I don't care." Then they leave.

Another respondent summarized,

> [A] lot of our concept planning projects don't have a specific construction schedule. It's really hard to motivate people to get engaged and involved. If it's construction and they know it's imminent and something's going to happen soon, then they show up.

The second difficulty created by hang time is that later in the lifecycle when detailed plans are released, citizen interest is increased but the key design decisions may well have already been made long ago. Revisions at this stage can be costly. However, citizens tend to focus on such decisions because the outcome will be sooner than was the case in an earlier stage. An interview respondent, a transportation engineer, stated,

> When it's a year or two years away a lot of people just don't show up. And then as we get down into preliminary engineering we hear a lot [of], "Well, when did you decide this?" "Two years [ago]." All of a sudden when people see the maps in the paper and [they think], "Holy cow, this is near my area." Now they start showing up. And you wish some of these people [with] good ideas would've showed up at an earlier phase, maybe at the Concept or Strategy stage, but they show up when it's more immediate to them. A challenge is to try to get early involvement.

The third difficulty that arises from the problem of hang time is that public attitudes toward a project are subject to change over time because of shifting economic or social conditions. In addition, the project parameters may alter over the course of a project due to similar shifts in economic or environmental conditions.

Participant Churn. A phenomenon related to hang time is participant churn. Citizens typically participate at different stages in a project's lifecycle. As a consequence, the views of those ultimately affected by decisions made during the Design phase may be very different from the views of those who were consulted at the Concept phase. Previously active citizens may have left the affected neighborhood or leadership of community groups may have changed. New leaders bring different priorities and mandates related to particular projects. If a project's hang time is more than, say, five years, participant churn is inevitable.

Turnover of citizen participants was mentioned by an interview respondent, who stated,

> It's always a challenge in communities to have a constant [representation] of people. The turnover in the communities is high. So you get community leagues, they get a different set of people every year sometimes and I've got a four- or five-year project. Actually, if you start from strategic level to finishing we're talking eight, ten years. So I think you have to continually test the opinions of those particular stakeholder groups and make sure that throughout the

course of the project that they're still onboard I guess. And part of that is making sure that they're informed.

Participant churn is not associated only with citizen participants. Through the stages of a project lifecycle, we can expect participant churn of the following: engineers, planners, administrators, elected representatives, and stakeholder groups.

Misaligned Expectations. When citizens learn at later stages in the lifecycle that they cannot change the main design elements of a project because of decision lock-in, they may feel dissonance because they realize that their expectation of strong influence in the design was not warranted. Had the same citizens been present at the Concept stage, they might have had a greater influence. The management problem of misaligned expectations sets in.

We point to two types of misaligned expectations. One concerns the timing of public involvement and the other the scope of public involvement. In terms of the misaligned expectations about timing, we have touched on this above in our discussion of decision lock-in, hang time, and participant churn. In terms of misaligned expectations about the scope of public involvement, citizens may expect broad scope for changes in a project, while the public-involvement process is designed for a much narrower scope. As one interview respondent noted,

> When we go and engage the public, it's raising expectations about what they might be able to participate in, and really it's mostly just public information sharing.

Another respondent commented,

> So we're in a little bit of a tight spot in our group. A lot of the times when we do go out for public involvement it's more as information sharing to let them know what we're building, and, of course, it's never taken that way.

Such misaligned expectations match the observations in a recent Public Involvement Audit (2014) for the City of Edmonton. The City Auditor observes

> [P]ublic involvement for some major capital projects takes the form of conveying information, rather than inviting a two-way exchange of information. . . There is a need in any municipal government to align the policies and practices of public involvement

Table 1.9 Recommendations for Challenge 6:

"In its public-involvement initiatives, municipalities are contending with the management problems of decision lock-in, hang time, participant churn, and misaligned expectations"
1. Specify priorities for public involvement by creating guidelines to support engagement planning for different types of projects across project lifecycles. Not all projects require the same level of public involvement. Specifying which projects require more in-depth public-involvement projects will allow for more predictable resource allocation and management of citizen expectations.
2. Develop procedures to guide the development, review, and approval of Public-Involvement Plans (PIPs). Such a process would include defining factors and circumstances that require the elevation of approval levels within organization. It would also define procedures and expectations for progress and evaluation of reports on public-involvement projects. In particular, it may be desirable to designate authority to a staff with engagement expertise to review and alter the scope of PIPs and develop procedures to guide the development, review and approval of PIPS.
3. Identify projects that would benefit from "public-involvement stewards" working with the projects over their entire lifecycles. This person or team would be responsible for ensuring that handoffs and updates are carried out seamlessly over the course of the project.
4. Enable information sharing and tracking as part of an effort to maintain an institutional memory of public-involvement processes over project lifecycles. Such a record could include transparent and prominent records of why particular decisions were made at each stage, recognizing input from citizens, and highlighting physical and logistical constraints. This could include electronic and physical templates.
5. Establish sunset clauses or other terms or conditions that would lead to a mandatory process review for projects. This would help ensure public-involvement work does not become outdated when implementation takes place. For example, if public involvement was done in the Concept phase and the project does not reach the Construction stage within five years, public involvement would need to be revisited and updated.
6. Develop and test innovative means to engage citizens in the Strategy and Concept stages. One example of this would be to design an interactive tool or game to support citizen involvement and understanding. A board game was developed by TransLink in British Columbia to involve citizens in planning future development of the system.
Long-term Excellence in Public Involvement
a. Assign staff members with expertise in public involvement to create dedicated, customized PIP forms, possibly customized to individual departments. The PIPs could have distinctive requirements in terms of the scope, role of technical information and knowledge, and outcomes for public-involvement initiatives.
b. Clearly define the municipality's relationship with its Community Leagues. This can be done by strategically supporting public-involvement activities that can be held under the auspices of the community leagues, as appropriate.

c. **Ensure clear accountability as defined by city policies, procedures, and bylaws.** It is often desirable for PIPs to be tested with small selections of stakeholders or prior to finalization. If applicable, the roles of the City Manager or Deputy City Manager should be specified.

d. **Use a Project Stage Indicator for Public involvement.** A Project Stage Indicator provides a unified visual and functional approach across municipal departments, helping decision-makers in various branches and departments communicate the stage of development of a project to citizens. Many cities at present do not use such a communications tool for communicating the stage of a project in its lifecycle, but it has proved useful for those that do. This tool can also facilitate keeping records of information learned from public involvement done in earlier stages.

e. **Use opportunities such as post-election City Council orientation sessions to ensure that information is shared periodically regarding key public-involvement events.** This would help to develop a dialogue among elected representatives and administrators in an effort to reduce misaligned expectations about the timing and scope for public-involvement projects.

with the expectations held by citizens and elected representatives. Contradictions exist between the expected nature and outcomes of public engagement and what actually takes place (Public Involvement Audit, May 22, 2014, 17).

The City Auditor's Report on Public Involvement (2014) identifies other areas in which the expectations of elected representatives for public involvement are not fully aligned with expectations of citizens, the most significant of which appears to relate to expectations of the scope of public involvement. City Council and administration in Edmonton expect public involvement to be used in instances in which public input can provide the greatest added value to a project, and public involvement is not envisioned for all projects.

Despite public expectations, current policy in Edmonton suggests judicious application of public involvement, stating "[p]ublic involvement processes will be designed to involve the appropriate people at the appropriate time in the appropriate way through the completion and communication of a public engagement plan for all processes" (Policy C513, 1). Similarly, the Guide for Project Managers (City of Edmonton, 2010), states "Public Involvement is pursued where there is a meaningful and explicit role for the public to add value to decision-making" (p. 1).

As a final issue for this section, relating to misaligned expectations, it is critical to manage "hand-offs" within a department or between city departments, as a project proceeds through its lifecycle. An example of how hand-offs can create problems is provided by one of the professionals we interviewed,

> I think what I'd like to have addressed is how the Transportation Planning group that does the overall Concept plan and is able to address the public concerns, how it can be easily passed onto us [Roads Department], because right now there is a large disconnect. When we go to the public we have to say, "The sidewalk's here because this other group told us it was going to be." There's a large amount of disconnect when we go out to the public, we don't have the freedom to be able to change things because it was already decided on previously.

In terms of the frequency of misaligned expectations, we observed that problems from misaligned expectations arose in five of the nine cases studies of this book. In four of these cases, the issues were significant enough to generate press coverage. This does not mean that more than half of the all projects in the department involve misaligned expectations. We selected cases to cover both controversial and noncontroversial projects, and to cover cases dealing with different constituencies, including individual citizens, various communities, businesses, and other organizations. Nevertheless, when we take into consideration the total number of major projects conducted in recent years relative to the number of projects covered in our case studies, it is clear that misaligned expectations occur periodically, and "citizen pushback" associated with misaligned expectations occurred at least once or twice a year in the recent past.

Challenge 7: Balance and Range of Public Perspectives

In its public-involvement initiatives, cities are not always able to acquire a balance and range of public perspectives.

> *The health of a democratic society may be measured by the quality of functions performed by private citizens.*
>
> —Alexis de Tocqueville

Project leaders necessarily must interpret and assess public input to provide a balance and range of perspectives to decision-makers. This may be a formal policy requirement. Edmonton Policy C513, for example, states that "a balance and range of public perspectives will be provided to decision makers for consideration in the decision process."

Acquiring such a balance and range of perspectives is a standard of practice that can be facilitated when planning the design of and using the results from public-involvement processes. However, it is desirable to reduce the amount of interpretation and assessment. This can be accomplished by seeking to optimize the diversity, range, and clarity of public contributions through explicit guidelines. Yet it is not easy to create effective and productive guidelines because acquiring truly representative input often requires sophisticated approaches and special skills.

Three general practices promote the acquisition of a balance and range of public perspectives: (1) ensure that a diverse population of affected citizens and stakeholders is identified and encouraged to provide input; (2) identify and remove systemic barriers to participation for excluded groups and those whose voices are routinely underrepresented; and (3) optimize the quality of input. These best practices are not easily realized, but improvements to existing practice should result in better public input, analysis, and reporting. (See Table 1.10 on pages 36-37 for specific recommendations.)

Reaching a Diverse Population. Many citizens and stakeholder groups are alert to and engage in public-involvement opportunities. However, some citizens and communities are neither alert nor engaged. Distance from political and policy discourse is a matter of choice for some. Many others are unaware of opportunities or insufficiently informed about how their interests are affected by emerging policy and project initiatives. Their lack of involvement skews participation and complicates efforts to meet desired standards of practice requirements.

One way of reaching diverse groups is by utilizing a variety of communication forms, including road signs, press releases and public relations, emails, flyers, advertising in print media, advertising on TV and radio, direct mail, social media, and advertising and promotions on the Web. By these methods many citizens will be informed in some fashion about public-involvement activities initiatives.

In communications, we found that often the following cohorts are heavily emphasized: general citizens, businesses, and community leagues, and other cohorts are much less targeted. A natural concern with such a broad focus is that important stakeholders and affected segments of the public may be unaware of involvement opportunities. Indeed, our in-depth interview commentary does suggest that partnering with community-league organizations is effective in reaching elements of the local citizenry, but not all, and perhaps especially not systemically excluded cohorts. Communications targeted at the general public undoubtedly penetrate so far. Tapping into discrete social networks that exist apart from the business community and community leagues to more fully communicate involvement opportunities appears to be important.

Interview respondents expressed concerns over their periodic inability to attract an adequate turnout to public-involvement events. There is value in high turnout and in a high response rate to general surveys. High turnout and high response levels can increase the probability that officials are exposed to diverse public perspectives. High turnout usually reflects a combination of heightened public awareness, interest, and mobilization that should elicit a broader range of opinion and interest. There are also political and event "theatrical" reasons for positively viewing and seeking to achieve high turnout and participation. Nonetheless, diversity and range of opinion are not necessarily affected by high turnout and high response rates, and representativeness certainly cannot be assumed to result. Seeking to maximize high turnout may actually result in lowering the ability of officials to acquire diverse and balanced input, a counterintuitive and unwelcome result. High turnout can obscure input from smaller and underrepresented cohorts and promote the tyranny of sheer numbers and of the loudest. These circumstances may undermine diversity and balance of opinion.

Given the virtues of high turnout it seems best for officials to pursue the objective. Nevertheless, formally structured efforts to acquire truly representative public input can enhance balance and diversity and can sharpen analysis. Officials can use representative sampling methodologies to select participants for workgroups, consultative meetings, citizen juries and forums, and surveys. Representative sampling methods promote acquisition of diverse and broad input and promote input that is most likely to hew closely to the affected population's perspectives. Representative sampling techniques, such as stratified sampling, may be too involved for run-of-the-mill involvement practice, but some consideration of representativeness is important. At the very least, staff should be able to acquire information on the basic social composition of communities and ideally about the structure of social networks and groups. This information can enhance understanding of who participates and who does not at open forums, group meetings, stakeholder involvement groups, and other more intimate gatherings. Such information should indicate which groups require special effort to reach.

Removing Barriers. In certain circumstances efforts beyond identification of affected publics are necessary. Groups of citizens may face systemic barriers to participation. Formal policy typically acknowledges as much: "where appropriate, processes [should be] used to include the public who need support to participate" (Policy C513). Conditions such as lack of mobility, temporal availability, poverty, low proficiency in English, distrust in or alienation from the political system, alternative cultural understandings of governance and citizenship, cultural prohibitions, and the ennui of youth can confound efforts to obtain input from segments of the public. It is necessary to address mobility barriers through proper selection of venues, to schedule involvement events at convenient times, and to employ interpreters in instances of anticipated need. Addressing social and cultural barriers can be more subtle.

Cultural knowledge of the excluded groups may be beyond the experience of project leaders and staff. Expecting staff to obtain such knowledge is probably unrealistic. Yet, to be successful in obtaining input from frequently excluded groups, cultural and social barriers must be appreciated and lowered. The surest ways to bridge cultural and social barriers is to acquire assistance from those who do understand these barriers and who can communicate with those who are excluded or whose voices are routinely underrepresented. It is also important for project leaders and others involved in receiving and analyzing inputs to understand the challenges of cross-cultural communications, possess knowledge of how to work with those who do possess cultural understandings, and have sufficient appreciation and skill to comprehend input. This requires diligence and patience.

Optimizing Inputs. Professionals carrying out public involvement are challenged in three principal ways in efforts to optimize quality input.

First, they must choose appropriate approaches and tools. Second, they must competently employ these approaches and tools. This includes addressing inherent limitations and common problems associated with the approaches and tools of choice. Third, they must accurately capture and interpret results.

In our research, the tool most frequently used consists of Open Houses, followed by Meetings with Stakeholders, Meetings with Community Groups, Collecting Surveys at Public Meetings, Workshops, Collecting Surveys Online, Use of Social media, and, to a lesser extent, Individual Interviews or Public Hearings at Council. It is unclear whether use of Social Media serves as a means of soliciting participation or as a venue for acquiring input—probably both.

Many interviewees find open houses valuable. Open houses reportedly achieve several things: less public surprise at construction, greater community understanding of a project, fewer public approaches to council members, and better departmental contact information available to the public. The focus is heavy on information provision and although information exchange occurs, open houses are reported to have limitations for consultation purposes and involved participation, and may elicit rushed and visceral (as opposed to reflective) contributions from citizens.

One limitation of open houses is that they possess relatively limited capacity to control for representativeness. In Edmonton, a Public Involvement Audit (May 22, 2014) suggested that open houses are the "default method" used in some City of Edmonton departments and that "there may be more appropriate methods" (p. i). If the goal is to acquire a range and balance of citizen perspectives, exclusive use of open houses may be suboptimal. We suggest that open houses be used in combination with other complementary approaches.

A distinction can be made between open houses on the one hand and, on the other, public forums and town halls, or similar open-invitation approaches in which a public exchange of views is featured. Such open forums, in which citizens provide officials with direct input on projects and initiatives, appear fairly common. Some interview respondents said that they found public forums and town halls flawed as approaches to capture balanced and diverse public input. Dominant speakers can express a narrow spectrum of opinion and, owing to their dominance, exclude or reduce expression of other perspectives. "Expert citizens" and others with broader agendas can capture or simply use these venues at platforms for their special interests. It is possible to have a tyranny of the majority in which minority opinion is submerged or debunked at the source.

Open forums can also be influenced by passions of the moment. It is commonly recognized (quite correctly) that "people who have strong opinions will use the town hall format to influence others" and that "town hall meetings have serious limitations because the opportunity for dialogue and discussion are extremely limited" (Involving Edmonton Handbook, p. 17). Nevertheless, perhaps counterintuitively, it is relevant that social science has long recognized the functionality of conflict. Ideational conflict within managed forums can define issues and sharpen perspectives. The energy of debate and dialogue or deliberation can bring new ideas and new voices to the table. These outcomes are valuable to optimizing clear input and to promoting a range and diversity of public perspectives. Open forums therefore have a place, although they should not be exclusively relied on for input. At two other extremes are more formal (one-way, or, push) communications strategies for information sharing and use of technology as a (two-way) public-involvement tool.

Achieving clarity of input is a two-way proposition. Citizens must be able to communicate their input, but it is also necessary for staff to comprehend the contributions so that they can accurately interpret and assess them. Basic listening skills are central to being able to effectively capture contributions. Officials should possess some combination of contextual and historical knowledge relating to the community and the project at hand. Improving community knowledge may involve simple practices such as producing more complete and structured project documentation or increasing assessment of sources and commentary that focus on communities and cohorts. Adopting best practices to ensure that important particulars and nuances are communicated between staff members when project responsibilities are handed off is another possible innovation. It is also important for municipal practitioners to confirm their understandings of public input.

Internal and External Inclusion. Finally, it is important to underline that including the excluded in public-involvement activities does not guarantee that they will be heard or can influence others. This difficulty is described

Table 1.10 Recommendations for Challenge 7:

"In its public-involvement initiatives, cities are not always able to acquire a balance and range of public perspectives"

1. Employ social-science methods drawn from marketing and social-network analysis to develop practical models of community social structures. These can provide guidance in identifying affected social networks and can facilitate acquiring a representative range of public opinion.

2. Create demographic-data resources and a geo-spatial map for the purpose of identifying networks of citizens who are least likely to participate in a public-involvement initiative. Open Government methods can also support this recommendation.

3. Tap the "street knowledge" of affected citizens and stakeholders through outreach efforts. This process could begin with city, business, and community-league sources, and extend to other known constituencies.

4. Ensure that stakeholder and community contact lists used are inclusive and reflect updated demographic information. These lists can be used to identify affected citizens.

5. Develop links and routinize communications with leaders of key social networks and stakeholder groups within communities. Work with leaders by identifying and developing information packages for different groups and sharing draft PIPs with them. Identify staff with appropriate cultural and social knowledge who can communicate with and promote sensitivity in engaging the participation of excluded and underrepresented groups.

6. Increase the capacity and knowledge of staff to appreciate, understand, and address systemic barriers to participation. As part of this effort, ensure that resources are allocated to identify and remove barriers and to support more diverse participation, such as providing child care, transportation, language translation, and having varied scheduling. Provide coaches for excluded and underrepresented groups so that they can more effectively provide input.

7. Encourage staff to use alternative or additional and complementary approaches to open houses with reference to the limitations of open houses to provide diverse public perspectives. Provide staff with knowledge, expertise, and encouragement to use an open public forum, instead of an open house.

8. Encourage use of a wide range of public-involvement approaches and tools. As part of this effort, new approaches and tools for public involvement can be promoted through a public-involvement community of practice (COP) (suggested under Challenge 4, recommendation 5, p. 19).

9. Routinize the best practice of returning to the public to clarify or confirm staff understandings of citizen contributions. The purpose of this practice is to increase the quality and clarity of information received from citizens. For return meetings with citizens, consider the use of controlled conflict and negotiation as techniques for facilitating input clarity.

10. Develop a procedure for determining when and how to use citizen juries, citizen panels, or other "representative sample" methods of involving the public. Such methods can be especially useful for generating citizen contributions on specific or technical issues.

Long-term Excellence in Public Involvement
a. Share resources developed within the organization corporate-wide.
b. In the PIP, include lines identifying Stakeholders Informed or Consulted, and justifying the proposed coverage of affected citizens, including the number of citizens planned to be reached in these groups. The PIP could also include a line discussing the selection and suitability of media to be used in the project.

as "internal exclusion." If the excluded are to have voice and to influence discourse they must possess the ability and opportunity to express their views. This suggests at least some form of development and coaching, and perhaps animation, is necessary. It will be difficult for project leaders themselves to build such competencies, but departments and cities have some responsibility if they are serious about obtaining input from the excluded. Project leaders do have the responsibility to be alert to internal exclusion and to see that efforts are made to capture the input and hoist perspectives that might otherwise be submerged or lost. This is true in open forums and also true when interpreting, assessing, and communicating input. To the extent that participation by the excluded is anticipated, project leaders should also plan involvement approaches that give the excluded opportunity for a stronger voice. Group meetings, individual interviews, and facilitated input in representative venues such as citizen juries can be used for this purpose.

Challenge 8: The public-involvement spectrum

Municipalities are finding that the public-involvement spectrum, while useful, requires selective and strategic use.

The improvement of understanding is for two ends: first, our own increase of knowledge; secondly, to enable us to deliver that knowledge to others.

—John Locke

Public-involvement projects can vary in size, significance, and complexity. When a public-involvement project is being designed, the public-involvement spectrum is often consulted. The spectrum was created by the International Association for Public Participation (IAP2). The continuum is a valuable tool for setting the public-involvement project in a context.

As often utilized, the spectrum's categories can be broken down as Sharing Information, Consultation, and Active Participation. From these categories, the practitioner must decide what level of public impact is being contemplated. (A more refined scale has five categories (see Figure 1.3). The original IAP2 version of the spectrum also describes public-involvement goals, commitment to the public, and sample techniques that are associated with varying design choices.) Questions can arise, however, in how the spectrum is interpreted and used.

Tension between standards and flexibility are unavoidable because, as an interview respondent noted:

> [B]y policy and best practice, we believe every PIP needs to reflect the specific circumstances of the situation. If it's infrastructure, for example, the tools and way we talk about LRT in Chinatown, and who we talk to, is very different than Millwoods. Very different contexts and needs. We develop standardized approaches (like the bike lanes have now), but they give us the ability to customize to the needs of projects.

How much public involvement is sufficient in a project is a pervasive question expressed by both interview and survey respondents. The extent of public involvement carried out can depend on the origins and objectives of a project. In particular, projects can start from within a Department, from an expressed public concern or outcry, from City Council, or from elsewhere within a municipality. Occasionally projects arise from needs identified through user surveys.

Survey respondents indicated that they found it difficult to match the public-involvement design, and its placement on the spectrum, with the scope and purpose of the project in its context. One survey respondent stated,

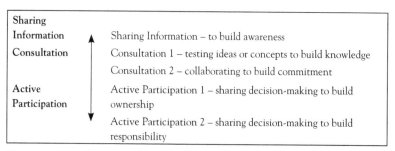

Figure 1.3. Public Involvement Spectrum

The purpose of the involvement and the scope of what is being consulted on should be more clearly defined. Maybe the consultation needs to begin earlier with an information session.

Matching the public-involvement project to an appropriate level on the spectrum, in particular, is difficult:

We don't necessarily have a procedure or a guideline that tells us exactly what to do. But we're starting to gain a lot of experience and that's helping us evolve to these new creative ideas. So I think in terms of an output it would be great to have something that's a little bit more tangible to say: maybe some kind of instructions that Council could provide, to say if you're working on this type of project this is where the bar is set. Because right now that bar is only set after the project is complete, and then somebody comes back and says you should have done this, and that's too late. So you need to set the bar at the front end of the project. It's challenging to do that.

Referring to the Walterdale Bridge case in this book, an interview respondent stated that matters related to the placement of the public-involvement project on the spectrum should have been determined at the beginning of the project lifecycle:

I think you want to try and settle upfront at the beginning where on this spectrum they are in terms of Consultation? Are they on the Information side? Generally, the public wants to be active participation on everything. I think at the front-end you've got to be specific about what is it that you can decide, have that conversation and understand maybe there's some concessions or some areas of decision-making that you can allow the public to have. Like, I don't want them designing the bridge.

As a rejoinder to the expressed desire for consistent application and clarity regarding public-involvement expectations of the City and the Department, some uncertainty may be unavoidable, as noted by another respondent:

[I]t's important to note. . .that [public-involvement] strategies are not political strategies. There will always be uncertainties and politicians will always react to their constituents. Basically, we can develop a 'standard plan,' and even set a target for participation. No one will care that we are following 'standards' when an issue pops up. They don't like it with engineering standards. It will certainly be an issue with involvement standards.

This leads to a phenomenon that we call "spectrum compression." This simply means that a large proportion of the public-involvement projects are at the Information level of the spectrum. More active levels of involvement for citizens, in the categories of Consultation and Active Participation can be rare. The category of "Active Participation - delegating decision making to build responsibility" often remains unutilized.

Evidence of spectrum compression in the City of Edmonton can be found in a sample of 21 Public-Involvement Plans (PIPs) that we reviewed. All twenty-one projects covered the Inform (information sharing)

Table 1.11 Recommendations for Challenge 8:

"Municipalities are finding that the public-involvement spectrum, while useful, requires selective and strategic use"
1. **Provide opportunities for in-depth public involvement by citizens in city planning.** Staff from various departments would engage periodically with citizens and stakeholders to identify top priorities for in-depth involvement on policies or projects. An example of an in-depth public-involvement process would be the Citizens' Panel on Edmonton's Energy and Climate Challenges. See http://www .edmonton.ca/city_government/environmental_stewardship/citizens-panel-energy-climate.aspx
2. **Create departmental guidelines to support planning for the depth of public involvement to be used.** Such guidelines would show how different types of projects should find an appropriate place on the spectrum.
Long-term Excellence in Public Involvement
a. **Create a city public-involvement handbook.** Such a handbook can include context and examples from various departments. One such handbook, for the City of Edmonton, is called *Involving Edmonton*. Guidelines for digital public involvement can also be helpful for administrators to capitalize on advantages and avoid limitations of digital methods.
b. **Involve citizens in the visionary elements of city planning.** The Burnham Plan of Chicago (1909) is an outstanding example of visionary planning. Such planning can be invigorated with modern public-involvement methods.
c. **Implement participatory budgeting.** Techniques and process for public involvement in budgeting have been refined in cities around the world, but few adopt the practice as a recurring annual event.

level of the spectrum. Then 19 of the 21 projects also covered of Consultation (testing ideas). But only 3 of the projects also covered the level of Consultation (to build commitment), only one project covered the category of Active Participation (to build ownership), and none of the projects involved Active Participation (with delegated decision-making).

This sample confirms that the Active Participation level of the spectrum is used infrequently in the City of Edmonton. This is not to state that there are no examples of Active Participation, but further exploration of spectrum compression could contribute to improved practice in public involvement. In other research, we have found that spectrum compression holds for other cities as well. To address this issue, we provide recommendations in Table 1.11.

Challenge 9: Closing the Loop with Citizens

Closing the information loop with citizens is emerging as a significant gap in public-involvement practice in municipalities.

> *Communication leads to community, that is, to understanding, intimacy, and mutual valuing.*
> —Rollo May, Psychologist

A public-involvement project is not finished until citizens are informed about the fate of their contributions in relation to decision-making. "Closing the loop" is critical for building trust, capacity, and a sense of legitimacy for citizens. Citizens must be informed about how their contributions made a difference. If decision-making was uninfluenced by citizen involvement, reasons should be stated. Closing the loop requires a clear evaluation strategy that tracks citizen contributions in relation to policy changes and decision-making, in concert with an effective communications strategy for sharing outcomes with citizens.

"Closing the loop" with citizens is widely considered a best practice. The IAP2 identifies it as one of the core values of excellence, stating, "Public participation communicates to participants how their input affected the decision." Similarly, the National Coalition for Dialogue and Deliberation (NCDD) states the principle that practitioners must,

Table 1.12 Recommendations for Challenge 9:

"Closing the information loop with citizens is emerging as a significant gap in public-involvement practice in municipalities"
1. **Close the loop with citizens.** Adopt the best practice of analyzing citizens' suggestions, and how these did or did not influence decision-making and policy (and why). Share this information with stakeholders. One useful tool is an "impact tree," which provides an overview of public input, overarching themes, and the impact on decisions. Potential overlaps and conflicts, and decision outcomes, including reasons.
2. **Close the loop with staff.** In this way, the successes of public involvement can become common knowledge and a point of pride.
3. **Close the loop with colleagues.** Consider sending delegates to the annual meetings of municipal associations to share learning and accomplishments.

"Ensure that each participatory effort has real potential to make a difference, and that participants are aware of that potential."

Our case studies suggest that closing the loop is not always consistent practice. One source stated, in regards to the case study about the Twin Brooks and Burnewood Area Projects:

> [T]hat's probably the one minor, I wouldn't say a failing. What I should say is we did let [citizens] know that we would be taking this before Council. We did notify them when the Council meeting was and told them that they could request to speak. But that was the extent of letting them know how that continues. So we really didn't close the loop. And you know maybe part of that was because there was no action out of it, but you're right, there was a little bit of a hole left there.

Another interviewee had similar views about the Bicycle Routes Public Involvement Case Study:

> One thing might be nice to get some feedback on about what we need to do a better job at I think is . . . going back to those communities and saying, "Here's what we implemented, here's the input we received from you, and here are some of the changes that we incorporated." I think that's something we need to improve on.

A survey respondent highlighted the importance of closing the loop with staff as part of the broad goal of maintaining positive relations with citizens:

We are the public face of the City when engaging citizens in these activities and asking for their input. If we have no intention of using the feedback in decision making in a way that we can communicate to the public, then we are put in a difficult position with respect to maintaining positive relations with the public when we seem to have just "gone through the motions."

Transparency is essential to the successful execution of a communications strategy. But it is even a more fundamental issue to the overall long-term success of public-involvement initiatives. Lack of transparency on the public-involvement process can dissuade citizens from participation, which in turn undermines the representativeness of those who participate. In this sense, pursuing the development of transparent processes for public involvement creates part of the infrastructure required for more successful inclusion of citizens in decisions that affect them (see Table 1.12).

Having provided an overview of nine key challenges to public involvement in this chapter, we now turn to nine case studies in this book that describe how city managers meet these challenges.

Suggested Readings

See Vargo, S. L., and Lusch, R. F. (2004). Evolving to a New Dominant Logic for Marketing. *Journal of Marketing*, 68(1), 1–17, for a discussion of co-creation of value. Also see Vargo, S. L. and Lusch, R. F. (2008). Service-dominant logic: Continuing the evolution. *Journal of the Academy of Marketing Science*, 36(1), 1–10.

The definition we use for public involvement on page 1 borrows from the City of Edmonton *Policy C513 (17 January 2006)*. The key motivation of this policy, stated therein, is that "The City of Edmonton believes that a key element of representative democracy is that people have a right to be involved in decisions that affect them." This, in turn, borrows, from the literature on public involvement. Regarding "closing the loop," C513 states, "Participants will know what is included in the discussion and what isn't, and what decisions will be made or have been made, and who will make the final decision." www.edmonton. ca/programs_services/documents/PoliciesDirectives/C513.pdf   Also see the Public Involvement Audit, May 22, 2014: www.edmonton. ca/city_government/documents/14370_Public_Involvement_Audit. pdf(accessed October 1, 2016)

PART 2

Case Studies in Public Involvement

CHAPTER 2

Twin Brooks and Burnewood Area Projects

Canceled after Public Consultations

Paul R. Messinger

In a departure from standard process for most projects, the Edmonton City Council made the budget allocation decision for these two neighborhood projects contingent on positive public consultation results. The two projects had been proposed by an external consultant to reduce the average speed of motorized vehicles by using a traffic circle, pedestrian crossing points, vertical elevations (including speed bumps), and other road modifications in two southern neighborhoods of Edmonton, Twin Brooks, and Burnewood. After negative feedback from citizen stakeholders obtained in a series of public meetings, City Council decided not to fund the fairly expensive projects ($1 to $2 million in Twin Brooks and $750,000 in Burnewood).

Context and Catalyst

Local citizens "wanting their communities to be safe was a real catalyst," commented one transportation department official after citizen complaints were expressed to the Transportation Services Department and to members of the City Council. These concerns were substantiated by city reports about speeding in the relevant areas in Twin Brooks (between

9th Avenue and 12th Avenue) and Mill Woods (Burnewood area, Jackson Heights, at the fringe of Mill Woods on the south side of 44th Avenue and 44th Street, winding between 50th and 34th Streets).

Planning

An external consultant, hired by city council provided general recommendations for road modifications to change driver's speed behavior, including a traffic circle, speed tables (raised areas), pedestrian crossings, and widened curbs to change drivers' speed behavior. The Transportation Services Department developed concepts for these two particular neighborhood areas following the consultant's recommendations to achieve the objective of reducing speed, danger, and risk of injury or death. A Transportation Services Department official described some of the proposed changes:

> So this is just the design realm and then we had a few speed tables . . . which are just little vertical elevations over an area that [the] consultant recommended in general or could be combined with say a pedestrian crossing point. So it was taking those combinations of features and looking at appropriate spacing to design it all over the road in hopes of bringing that average speed that drivers drive the road down. That's the concept of it.

A nonstandard process was put in place whereby public engagement would be carried out, and a detailed implementation plan and budget would be developed by the Transportation Services Department and considered by City Council, contingent on the outcomes of the public-involvement process. This departs from the standard city design and implementation process [see p. 23, Figure 1.2], where, first, a concept plan is developed by Transportation Services, together with a proposed budget. If City Council approves the plan and budget, then a detailed design and implementation plan would be developed and carried out.

The standard process typically involves a four-year cycle (previously a three-year cycle), with public consultation occurring at each stage, particularly the concept and the design stages, but with the public consultation for the design stage just for the purpose of getting input on and making modifications to the design (not for rejecting the project). In this case, because of some combination of this coming from an outside consultant's report commissioned by City Council and the high project costs, there was a departure from the standard process, whereby more detailed design elements were included in the initial concept plan. This concept plan was vetted through public involvement prior to the budget being passed, and the time frame for this public involvement (PI) was compressed because of the desire of City Council to act quickly.

> The cost estimates I believe for Twin Brooks were between $1 and $2 million and Burnewood was about $750,000 to make these changes on the roads. And it's those scale of costs that really required us to ask for, you know this was outside our normal process so we needed to go and ask council for money to do these . . . So it really was council that was the catalyst that started us down the path of exploring ways for the roads that we saw were the biggest issues in the city to try and help more than we had previously done. So we were really asked by council to explore this and to make the allocation of budget contingent on PI, in a nonstandard process.

> I should mention that we actually compressed the timelines that are recommended . . . because of when we had to get back to Council, I think . . . we usually like to have about half a year to make sure that we give time for the community, we get a good venue, we get time to get the message out, and then we get time to do our feedback. And we had to compress this in half, and this was kind of, we fast tracked this process in case Council wanted to proceed on this.

Engagement

Public meetings were called for the two neighborhoods, planned to last for two to three hours. Portable boards and leaflets were used to publicize the meetings, and stakeholders were contacted, including community leagues, community organizers, and school administration. Lead time of about three months was given in planning and publicizing the meetings, rather than the more standard six months.

At the meetings, the detail plans were displayed and participants could place sticky notes with their comments on the plans. A website was set up, and people at the meetings were encouraged to post feedback on the website and send emails for up to one week after the public meetings. The electronic means of communication turned out to generate 1.5 to 2 times as many responses as the in-person feedback provided at the meetings.

> We had people from our office of traffic safety that had helped support us on the data side of how we got to these roads. They reviewed collisions which were part of that check and they had all the speed information and then there was . . . a staff member . . . that gave the presentation about the outcomes of those changes on the road that we proposed based on the study we had done.

Attendance was about 100 residents at the Twin Brooks meeting and between 25 and 40 residents at the Burnewood meeting. Response at the former meeting was mostly negative, and response at the latter meeting was mixed (50/50 percent positive versus negative comments), with a number of neutral comments. Electronic follow-up was similar to the in-person comments at the first meeting concerning the Twin Brooks plan and somewhat more negative than the in-person comments concerning the Burnewood plan.

Impact

After reviewing the public consultation feedback from the two communities, together with the concept plan and budget, the City Council decided to cancel both plans. A Transportation Services Department official summarized the outcome:

> Next step is going to City Council and letting them debate and discuss if they think there's value for the cost we found, the feedback we got from the community to ask us to proceed further to do the design, or the implementation. Go to the next level which is detail design, or we might go out to the field,

survey it, get the exact dimensions and start deciding how to actually physical[ly] build and cost out building this. And City Council told us this seems to be too expensive to do as an independent road especially given the mixed reviews we got from the community. So it's expensive, community didn't seem to really think it was a good idea for their community, I think we'll have you stop there and not proceed further. So that's basically what happened.

Closing the loop: In this case, public consultation led to the outcome preferred by the majority of residents who participated, but this fact was not directly communicated to residents that participated in the public engagement activities:

> . . . we did notify them when the Council meeting was and told them about their, what the public can do to request to speak, and we informed them about what that was gonna be, but that was the extent of engagement on letting them know how that continues. So we really didn't close the loop.

Those residents who attended would have been pleased that their views had been heeded. Some residents would have read about this in the news media or heard from friends who attended, and all residents would have eventually noted that no construction occurred. No direct communication was made to residents through the same channels as the public consultations, that the plans had been dropped and that their views were an important factor.

Assessment and Learning

This public engagement process seemed to function well on several grounds: the public was listened to and money was not spent on projects that residents did not want. Still planning officials in the Transportation Services Department appeared disappointed that much work went into a project that was dropped—a project which, on technical considerations, could increase public safety and reduce noise.

In my mind it may have been smarter to have that discussion with Council and say here's what it's going to cost to do, do you feel this is worthy of proceeding further? If they thought it was, then part of the process should've been then to go to the community and say 'we have funding support for this and we wanna do this, what do you think?' Because we kind of went in and we took people's time, we got them out to this meeting and told them 'we might do this if we get money, what do you think?' And to me there may have been a little bit more solid process if we would've done it in a different order.

On reflection, at least two important open questions were raised by a Transportation Department official.

1. What is the value of time spent on public involvement? As one official mentioned, "[W]hat's the value in using that information to help in a positive way [to] influence our decisions and outcomes?"
2. How much public involvement is enough? How many people should be contacted? How does a municipal department make the case that it has contacted "representative" people? "[A]nother thing is from a research perspective when do we and when can we say independently outside of the expectations of Council that we have effectively engaged the majority of the public? To me that's another big question that we really need to talk about, because there's a perspective out there that you may have done better but you still haven't quite done good enough, you haven't quite got to enough people, or you haven't really represented the people you should've engaged."

Sources

Compiled from interview responses of participants involved with this case and the Edmonton Transportation Service Department's Public Involvement Plan (PIP).

CHAPTER 3

Edmonton's Walterdale Bridge

Fait Accompli

Heather Stewart and Paul R. Messinger

The Walterdale Bridge replacement project conducted public involvement that generated high levels of both participation and controversy. Four design options were presented to the public in 2010 for idea testing at well-publicized open houses, as per the Public-Involvement Plan (PIP).[14,1] However, some participants felt that they had missed out on opportunities to participate in developing those four options, and were frustrated that little leeway existed for solutions outside of those four preselected options.[12] Magnified by the importance of the River Valley area to Edmontonians and a history of insensitive management of First Nations burial sites, this frustration grew into social media campaigns by some residents to "save" the bridge.[10,11] After one of the designs was approved by council (see Figure 3.1), significant public involvement continued throughout Preliminary Engineering, including a Stakeholder Input Group and significant consultation with First Nations groups.[2,4]

The city was successful in promoting opportunities for stakeholders to participate and in generating a great deal of participation. Given the sensitivity of the subject, not everyone could be in agreement with the outcome. However, assessment of the public-involvement process identified three main concerns (in ascending order) that will be valuable to consider for future projects. First, some participants called for greater outreach for public involvement (PI) events and opportunities. Second,

Figure 3.1 Walterdale Bridge: Old (top left) and New (top right). *In the architectural rendering (bottom image), the planned new $155-million bridge is shown located several meters east (right) of the existing bridge (left, shown faintly) which will be removed once the new bridge is operational.*[3]

clearer explanations were needed to generate greater understanding of decision-making factors and processes. Third, some stakeholders called for more open-ended public consultation prior to narrowing down project options. The City has already made progress in piloting new approaches to address these concerns in subsequent projects and continues to evaluate ways to improve the public-involvement process for the future.[2,8,13]

Context and Catalyst[4,5,6,14]

The Walterdale Bridge was built between 1912 and 1913, opening the same year as Edmonton's High Level Bridge. The bridge was given a structural assessment in 2000 and rehabilitated to serve until 2015. As early as 2002, the City of Edmonton's commissioned assessments have been counting down to the end of the Walterdale Bridge's useful life as a vehicular bridge.

Again in 2008, a bridge condition assessment concluded that the bridge needed replacing, and City Council began moving forward on replacement planning.

The Walterdale Bridge is a green steel truss structure with three humps, an artifact of the city's industrial past. Detractors point to its utilitarian structure, deterioration, and noise, while admirers praise its connection to Edmonton's industrial past, its historic age, and its distinctive hum.

The crossing is complicated by history. The bridge replaced the previous Walter ferry service. Its northern base is located in the neighborhood now known as Rossdale, near the original Hudson's Bay Company Fort Edmonton site, which was in turn built at the site of a millennia-old meeting place for multiple First Nations on traditional territory of the Papaschase people, who were displaced multiple times by Hudson's Bay and City of Edmonton expropriations. The old EPCOR power plant was built nearby. Only after the late 1990s, after a century of development and backfill, was that site recognized as an ancient First Nations burial ground. This history set the stage for First Nations distrust in future planning processes.[6,11]

Edmontonians tend to regard the River Valley as a feature central to the identity of the city. Any development that impacts the River Valley, including bridges, is potentially sensitive.

The planning was conducted with reference to existing Strategic Plans and policies, including the City of Edmonton Policy on Public Involvement, the West Rossdale Urban Design Plan, active transportation assessments, and more.

An independent Urban Design Salon event in March 2008 discussed possibilities including retaining the old bridge as a nonvehicular multiuse route alongside a new "signature" bridge. This idea-generating event foreshadowed the coming controversy with the following statement: "Early public support is important for such a venture and clear facts combined with significant tangible benefits, such as the amenities discussed, can make the bridge an easier sell."[9]

Prior to the public-involvement activities there were invitational stakeholder scoping meetings. Stakeholder representatives were not allowed to share what they heard at the meeting with their constituents, which created some tension.[15]

Planning[1,2,4]

The City of Edmonton hired Gray Scott Consulting Group to manage the public-involvement process for the Walterdale Bridge in partnership with ISL Engineering/Al-Terra Engineering. A PIP was developed and approved in summer 2010 for the Concept Planning study. The Level of Involvement was Sharing Information to Build Awareness (Information Sharing) and Testing Ideas or Concepts to Build Knowledge (Consultation, level one). Information sharing included information on construction impact and safety. Idea testing meant that a series of possible choices would be presented to the public to determine preferences. (For background on the public involvement spectrum, see p. 38.) Ideas for testing included the following:

- High-level criteria for evaluating bridge design options;
- "Signature" bridge design options;
- Strategies to address vehicle access/egress to communities/institutions;
- Pedestrian/cyclist circulation impacts and mitigations; and
- Visual integration of the replacement bridge and the associated roadway network.

The PIP identified outreach plans for participant outreach including major adjacent landowners, stakeholder groups, community leagues, and institutions (including aboriginal and Métis groups). It also detailed the types of events, including one-on-one meetings, small group meetings, public workshops, and public information sessions.

Engagement[1,2,4,5,16,17]

Over 400 people participated in over 20 public-involvement events between May 2010 and April 2011. In addition to Gray Scott Consulting Group, ISL Engineering and Al-Terra Engineering are mentioned in the PIP. Dialog consulting architects and the City of Edmonton staff were involved in leading this three-phase Concept Design public-involvement process.

Phase I (individual interviews, discussions, and meetings) was held in summer 2010; Phase II (open houses and questionnaire collection) was held in Fall 2010; and Phase III (information sessions to present the final Concept Plan recommendations to the public) was held in March 2011.

Following the Concept Design approval by City Council, the Preliminary Engineering design phase began which included further public-involvement activities:

- Fall 2011: Stakeholder interviews;
- December 8, 2011: Stakeholder Input Panel Meeting #1;
- February 8, 2012: Public Information Session #1;
- May 28, 2012: Stakeholder Input Panel Meeting #2;
- January 23, 2013: Stakeholder Input Panel Meeting #3; and
- February 7, 2013: Public Information Session #2.

Impact[2,4,7,8,13,14]

Feedback gathered in Concept Planning public-involvement phases I and II were balanced against technical analysis and strategic priorities in order to rank a range of four preselected bridge design options and related considerations, and select final recommendations.

Six common feedback themes involved the need to do the following:

- Respect the environment and context of the area;
- Minimize impacts to historical and cultural resources and treat cultural resources with respect;
- Provide access to commercial, recreational, residential, and other roads;
- Maintain/improve pedestrian and cyclist connections through area;
- Protect safety, integrity, and character of adjacent neighborhoods; and
- Reduce disruption during construction (traffic delay/detouring, noise, and so on).

Four competing feedback themes, which required balancing, were:

- Signature Bridge versus Cost;
- Improve Traffic Flow, Operations, and Geometry versus Minimize Impact to Parks and Environment;
- Two-way Traffic versus Cost, Community Impacts, and Traffic Impacts; and
- Improve Traffic Flow, Operations, and Geometry versus Community Impacts.

As an *Edmonton Journal* article summarizes, "In 2010, four designs were proposed, and after several consultations with the public and stakeholder groups, the city decided to go with the most ambitious proposal—the arch bridge, a design not seen before in the river valley. It was chosen over more simplistic styles, such as a girder bridge like the High Level Bridge, due to several factors, including aesthetics, environmental concerns, and lifecycle costs. In April 2011, city council approved the design.

"At that time, a concept-level proposal for the three-lane arch bridge was estimated at $132 million, which was $43 million more than a two-lane girder bridge. After receiving bids from four contractors, the city selected the lowest offer, awarding the project to Vancouver-based Spanish company Acciona/Pacer Joint Venture. However, the bid was still 14 per cent more than earlier estimates, bringing the price tag of the Walterdale Bridge up to $155 million."[14]

Further input to Preliminary Engineering public involvement included the development of a stakeholder input panel, further stakeholder consultation and a public open house between 2011 and 2013. Public involvement in this project phase addressed "final bridge design, alignment, construction lay-down areas, associated road and trail connections, utility relocations, and requirements to protect cultural heritage and the environment."[7]

Assessment and Learning[2,12,13]

Three key learnings were noted by City staff and documents following the Walterdale Bridge PI process. Greater outreach was needed for PI events and opportunities, clearer explanations were needed for project decision-making factors and processes, and finally there was strong public demand for more open-ended public consultation prior to narrowing down project options.

The Walterdale Bridge Public Involvement Report noted feedback suggestions that some "respondents felt there should have been more information provided about the process itself, and how and when to participate," and that a "segment of the population would like a more active role in the decision-making process." The Report notes that "the process was not designed nor intended to collaborate with community and stakeholders to determine a recommended route." The concept of whether to have a signature bridge was also not open for consultation, only expression of preferences for one style of signature bridge or another. Feedback forms suggested that around 10 to 15 percent of respondents had negative views about the public-involvement process.[2]

Following the public involvement activities, some citizens felt that their preferred options had never been presented for consideration, including preserving the historic bridge as a pedestrian-cycling route instead of demolishing it and including a new multiuse route alongside the new bridge.[10] Others were opposed to the concept and cost of a signature bridge.[2] Some observers were critical of the public-involvement process.[12] Finally, some First Nations groups remained unsatisfied with City plans for addressing the ancient burial grounds.[11] These concerns have been expressed in blogs, Facebook Pages such as "Save the Walterdale Bridge" and newspaper articles.[10,14]

The weakness of the Walterdale Bridge public-involvement process was not in actual outreach and event promotion, but in the public perception that they may have missed opportunities for contributing to preliminary concept design planning, when in fact those opportunities never existed. Instead, the City started Phase III of the public-involvement process by offering four preset design options. Although the outreach and stakeholder involvement was thorough, the options presented were limited and people already felt that their hands were tied and that very few of their own ideas could be considered. Participants felt that they had missed out on (or been excluded from) earlier public consultations, but in fact the four design options were created mainly by the consulting engineering firms and the Transportation Department. The public involvement activities were never designed to do more than "test ideas," that is, select between a set of predrafted concept designs. Some of the residents became increasingly anxious and discontented when they realized how far along the process was.

The higher-than-usual level of public-involvement activities into the Preliminary Engineering and Construction phases of the project reflect the sensitivity of the project to the public, City Council, and the Transportation Department.

One interpretation of the way the City of Edmonton responded to these criticisms in its public-involvement approach is captured in an interview conducted for a City of Edmonton Transportation Public Involvement Review:

> "[The City of Edmonton] had done a concept plan for . . . the replacement of Walterdale Bridge and the realignment of it. And one of the things that we found through that study and through a number of other studies prior to that was that . . . stakeholders and City Council were not understanding why we were getting to the answers that we were getting to. And so when we were developing [a new Public Involvement Plan] that was something that was really quite important to us, we wanted to make sure that our stakeholders and council could understand the process from start to finish and that we weren't going in with a preconceived plan— 'This is the plan,' and 'shoving it down their throats' as we've been told in a number of cases."[13]

These reflections have been applied to some newer public-involvement projects, notably the 149th Street Interchange project [see pages 79-82], which collected public feedback prior to developing a preliminary concept plan based on that feedback and technical specifications. This approach addresses the concerns of the Walterdale Bridge participants and can help identify major concerns and stakeholder priorities early in the process, thereby avoiding costly conflict resolution further down the line. However a more open-ended public-involvement approach is more labor-intensive and time-consuming, and it does not eliminate the potential for disagreement and controversy. The City is working to determine the most effective tools and processes for public involvement in projects of varying levels of sensitivity and impact. [13,16,17]

Postscript

The bridge, originally scheduled to open in Fall 2015, is now expected to open midway through 2017. A timeline of relevant events is provided in the *Edmonton Journal*:[18]

April 2011: Edmonton city council, led by then-mayor Stepen Mandel, chooses a design for a new Walterdale Bridge. Council opts for the most expensive, ambitions, and difficult of four shortlisted designs. The proposed bridge has an estimated budget of $132 million.

May 2013: The city awards the contract to Vancouver office of Spanish construction giant Acciona S.A., which partners with Pacer Corp. of Calgary. Acciona/Pacer Joint Venture beats out local firms including PCL. Acciona/Pacer has the lowest bid, based in part on its partnership with South Korea's Daewoo steel company, which provides steel at lower prices than Canadian companies. Despite accepting the lowest bid, the total cost of the project goes up 14 per cent, to $155 million. The bridge is scheduled to open in autumn of 2015.

May 2014: Steel to build the bridge arches scheduled to arrive in Edmonton. The steel does not arrive. A new target date is assigned: December 2014.

January 2015: The city confirms that the steel, now six months late, has still not arrived. The city says the steel will arrive in February or March, but that the bridge will still open on time.

April 2015: Six months before bridge is scheduled to open, the city announces 20 of the needed 42 steel segments that will form bridge arch have still not arrived from South Korea. Deck steel has also not arrived. In all, 60 to 70 per cent of the necessary steel is still not here for the 2015 construction season. The city estimates the bridge will now open in autumn of 2016.

June 2015: Acciona/Pacer begins accruing late penalties of $10,000 a day.

July 2015: Efforts to float the steel arches down the North Saskatchewan bog down because of unusually low water levels.

August 2015: After the city dredges the river, steel pieces are able to float down the North Saskatchewan to the construction site.

March 2016: Subcontractor Capitol Steel files a lawsuit against Acciona/Pacer alleging that the South Korean steel pieces had defective welds, coating damage, distortion and gaps. Capital alleges Acciona/Pacer wanted them to make up lost time by doing substandard repairs. In a counter-claim, Acciona/Pacer called the Capitol Steel suit "frivolous and improper." It counter-sues for $16.7 million, alleging Capital Steel overcharged for its repair work and delayed construction by forcing Acciona/Pacer to hire a new contractor. The city insists its own third-party engineers are providing rigorous quality control.

June 2016: Construction begins on the main bridge deck.

September 2016: The city announces that the bridge will not open this fall, but sometime midway through 2017, citing delays in completing construction of the deck before the onset of winter.

Oct. 31, 2016: Acciona/Pacer Joint Venture will see its late penalties rise to $17,000 a day.

Edmonton Journal columnist Paula Simons quotes Adam Laughlin, deputy city manager of integrated infrastructure services,

> "It's a pretty complex, iterative process," says Laughlin . . . "We need to do a better job of managing expectations," he says. "Construction is not an exact science. It's unrealistic to expect every project will be on time and on budget."

Simons concludes, "Perhaps, next September, when (and if) we drive across our elegant swooping bridge, we'll forget our frustrations, and rejoice that we do have a unique piece of urban architecture.

"But right now, it's hard not to feel that we've been upsold, yet again, by a City Hall that over-promises, that falls in love with dream projects that prove harder to make reality."[18]

Sources

1. City of Edmonton Walterdale Bridge Public Involvement Plan 2010.

2. City of Edmonton Walterdale Bridge Public Involvement Report 2011 www.edmonton.ca/documents/PDF/Walterdale_Bridge_Public_Involvement_Report.pdf (accessed on October 1, 2016).

3. Upper left: en.wikipedia.org/wiki/Walterdale_Bridge#/media/File: Walterdale_bridge_from_below.jpg; bottom left: www.dialogdesign .ca/projects/walterdale-bridge-replacement; and right: www.youtube .com/watch?v=j5IafTmpL-c (approximately second 0:34 of 2.26 video). (All three URLs accessed on October 1, 2016).

4. Walterdale Bridge Replacement and Approach Roads Evaluation Concept Planning Study Final Report April 2011. www.edmonton. ca/documents/RoadsTraffic/110504-Walterdale-Bridge-Replacement-and-Approach-Roads-Evaluation-CPS-Final-Report-1.0.pdf (accessed on October 1, 2016).

5. The Way We Move Walterdale Replacement Bridge FAQ, www .edmonton.ca/documents/WalterdaleBridge_UpdateFAQ_07082015 .pdf (accessed on October 1, 2016).

6. The Way We Move Historical Resources Walterdale Bridge FAQ www .edmonton.ca/documents/RoadsTraffic/H3-WalterdaleBridge_ HistoricalResourcesFAQ_08022012.pdf (accessed October 1, 2016).

7. Walterdale Bridge Replacement Detailed Design Update (June 2012). www.edmonton.ca/documents/PDF/Walterdale_Bridge_Update_-_ June_2012.pdf (accessed October 1, 2016).

8. Walterdale Bridge Replacement Project Update (December 2012) www.edmonton.ca/documents/PDF/Walterdale_Design_Update_ Dec_12.pdf (accessed October 1, 2016).

9. Bridging the Gap: Improving Traffic, Tourism and Civic Identity in Edmonton's Core, *AACIP Planning Journal*, Winter 2009, Alberta

Association, Canadian Institute of Planners. www.albertaplanners.com/sites/default/files/PDFS/PlanJournalMar09.pdf(accessedOctober1,2016).

10. Save The Walterdale Bridge Facebook page www.facebook.com/SaveTheWalterdaleBridge (accessed October 1, 2016).

11. CTV Edmonton Dec. 29 2012 "First Nations against Walterdale Bridge project" edmonton.ctvnews.ca/first-nations-against-walterdale-bridge-project-1.1095381 (accessed October 1, 2016).

12. MasterMaq Blog Mar. 23 2011 "The City of Edmonton is failing at public involvement" blog.mastermaq.ca/2011/03/23/the-city-of-edmonton-is-failing-at-public-involvement (accessed October 1, 2016).

13. Interview by authors with a City of Edmonton Transportation Services Department official.

14. *Edmonton Journal*, Nov. 2, 2013 "Walterdale Bridge - Step by step: How the bridge is being built" www.edmontonjournal.com/news/insight/walterdale-bridge/index.html#sthash.3YuVVYWu.dpuf (accessed on October 1, 2016).

15. Discussion notes from June 6, 2014 Advisory Council Meeting for Centre for Public Involvement Transportation Public Involvement Review project.

16. www.edmonton.ca/projects_plans/walterdale_bridge/project-history-concept-phase.aspx (accessed on October 1, 2016).

17. www.edmonton.ca/projects_plans/walterdale_bridge/project-history-design-phase.aspx (accessed on October 1, 2016).

18. *Edmonton Journal*, September 24, 2016 "City Over-Promised on 'Signature' Bridge", p. A4. http://edmontonjournal.com/opinion/columnists/paula-simons-troubled-bridge-over-walterdale-waters (accessed on October 1, 2016).

CHAPTER 4

Valley Line Expansion, Public Involvement, and Sad Don

Heather Stewart and Paul R. Messinger

Project management of even one leg of one line of light rail transit (LRT) expansion is extremely complex, involving a large stable of outside consultants and city staff, and this expansion, part of a near doubling of the LRT coverage, was no exception (see Figure 4.1). Concomitant with the scale of the project, there was extensive engagement of the public. And there is a wealth of evidence showing the many ways that participant feedback has been incorporated into designs. But a review of reports and media also reveals processes that are occasionally inconsistent in style and detail, perhaps owing to the wide scope of activities. There was a visible learning curve in responses by public-involvement spokespersons to critical media coverage. Some early media quotes could have been interpreted as dismissive, while later in the process a more polished approach emerged. Documentation of the process was detailed, perhaps even overwhelming for department users and stakeholders. Much of the evaluation process appeared to focus on compiling comments from feedback forms, rather than providing a coherent synthesis.

Due to the size and cost of this project, public goodwill—or occasional lack of it—has had a direct impact on the financial viability of the project and the associated influence on provincial and federal funding decisions. While the overall outcomes for public goodwill and intergovernmental funding have been positive, this experience illustrates the need for a consistent and clear engagement process for long-term projects.

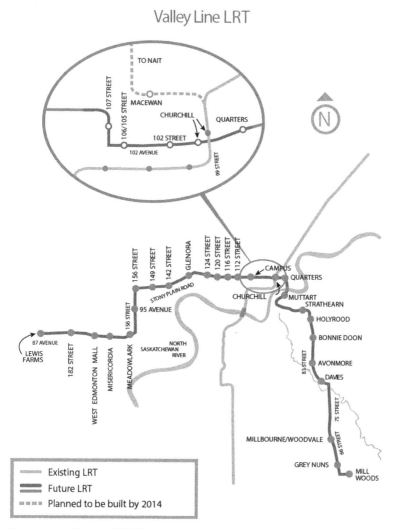

Figure 4.1 Planned LRT expansion

And while not part of the formal engagement process, a particularly note-worthy episode in this history was the adroit use of social and traditional media to mobilize grassroots support for funding at the provincial level.

Context and catalyst

LRT line expansion has been discussed in Edmonton for decades, going back to 1977 when the City of Edmonton approved a southeast LRT leg to Mill woods, at a projected cost of $101 million, but which was never built.[31] The idea for expansion was revived in response to a growing urban population and following the development of the City's "The Way Ahead" Strategic Vision, the "Way We Grow" municipal development plan, the "Way We Move" transportation plan, and the LRT Network Plan.[3]

Planning

The SE-West LRT Expansion is being conducted in five phases:[5]

Strategy: Conducted in and prior to 2009, the strategic plans guiding the city's goals toward 2040 include the Municipal Development Plan, the Transportation Master Plan, and the LRT Network Plan.[23,8] The public was consulted through public involvement (PI) activities including surveys.[1]

Concept: Corridor Definition and Concept Planning, each with their own public-involvement processes, were conducted in 2009 to 2010. A public-involvement plan (PIP) devoted to Concept Planning was developed in March 2009.[4]

Design 2011 to 2016: This phase includes Preliminary Engineering and Detailed Engineering, with a PIP[7] detailing information sharing, idea testing for options in structural aesthetics, LRT stop/station aesthetics, landscaping, public art, transportation network connectivity, noise, and mitigating impacts, as well as active involvement in sound attenuation decision-making. This phase of public involvement was planned to include five stages:[9]

> Design Stage 1: Pre-Consultation (Nov 2011 to Feb 2012),
> Design Stage 2: Initiation (Feb to May 2012),
> Design Stage 3: Consultation (May to Dec 2012),
> Design Stage 4: Refinement (Sept 2012 to June 2013),
> Design Stage 5: Conclusion (Jan to Oct 2013).

This phase also included costing and funding plans, which in this case involved extensive public-advocacy initiatives including #yeg4LRT in 2013 to 2014.

Build: The construction *phase of the project is planned to run from 2016 to 2020 through a private contractor.* [17]

Operate: Active operation of the Valley Line is planned from 2020 to 2050 through a private contractor firm running low-floor LRT trains integrated with the rest of the otherwise publicly operated LRT network.[13]

Engagement

The public was engaged in several phases:

Corridor Selection

The SE-W corridor selection phase was facilitated by CH2M HILL consultants and representatives from multiple City of Edmonton branches. The process included three elements: Technical Studies, Public Input, and the development of the overall LRT Network Plan which included the SE-W corridor.[3]

In the public-involvement phase, "a total of 3,811 participants contributed to the public involvement process for both West and Southeast LRT in 2009. Over 94 public involvement activities were held, including questionnaires, workshops, online consultation, stakeholder interviews/meetings, and open houses."[3]

Concept Planning

Over 700 people participated[6] in the Concept Planning public-involvement Information sharing and idea-testing engagement on LRT Alignment, stations configuration, vehicle access, pedestrian/cyclist impacts, parking, and visual integration. This process shared information and tested ideas using individual and group stakeholder meetings and interviews, a series of neighborhood workshops, open houses, and a final presentation of the Recommended Concept Plan.[4]

Line Names

A concurrent public-involvement process gathered public feedback as one input toward naming decisions for the expanded multiline Edmonton LRT system. Over 3,000 names were submitted, shortlisted by the City, and sent to market research in 2012. The City of Edmonton Naming Committee then used the market research recommendations to approve five names in early 2013, including the name "Valley Line" for the SE to West route.

Design

The Preliminary Design process carried out five stages of public consultation, as initially planned. But only Stage 4 (Refinement) included an online report with participation numbers, showing four neighborhood-specific meetings with a total of 460 participants. This variation in reporting may be related to the broad group of leading consultants involved in the process, which have formed the "connectEd Transit Partnership" comprised of AECOM, Hatch Mott MacDonald, DIALOG, ISL, GEC, and various other specialized consultants.[22]

Impact

Corridor Selection

Based on data collected, city administrators screened a shortlist of potential corridors using the criteria of Feasibility, Environment and Community, and the shortlist was then evaluated against a Council-approved rubric of weighted factors to select a final preferred corridor.[21]

When representatives from the community opposed the preferred 87th Avenue corridor route during public consultations run by Kaleidoscope Consulting, the spokesperson for the process clarified the purposes of public involvement, reminding the public that "The current process is not meant to have stakeholders vote yes or no on the LRT line . . . but to inform them and listen to them."[2] Ultimately the 87th Avenue corridor was approved.

Concept Planning

According to the PIP, "Information from public involvement will be shared with the project team, to be considered along with technical findings and as an input into the technical evaluation process. A summary of all public input will be shared with City Council for review when considering the West and Southeast LRT Concept Plans."[4] The Concept Plan was approved by City Council in January 2011. This included detailed plans of routes in specific neighborhoods. Specific impacts from public involvement were not identified, but plan highlights included the demolition and rebuilding of the Cloverdale footbridge into a combined two-level LRT/pedestrian bridge,[10] and the amendment in March 2012 which removed the previously approved Whitemud stop and replaced the Wagner stop with a revised Wagner station.[6] A citizen group called Save Edmonton's Downtown Footbridge organized to try to reverse plans to demolish the existing pedestrian bridge, calling the consultation process "vague" and "confusing".[20]

Line Names

The cost to come up with LRT line names including Valley Line was estimated at $20,000 to $30,000. Then-Councilor (now Mayor) Don Iveson explained that the public engagement process was also aimed at helping to generate public advocacy which could help the City to secure more transit funding from provincial and federal governments.[18]

Design[24]

The impact of Preliminary Design consultations is reflected in the public presentation of the recommended design.

Stops: Stakeholders confirmed themes for a variety of stop/station elements, such as benches and paving.

Shelter Canopies: Of three shelter canopy options, stakeholders preferred the organic shaped canopy.

Access to Businesses and Communities: Stakeholders value ease of access to businesses and community attractions for pedestrians, cyclists, and vehicles.

Bicycles: Stakeholders indicated they want bicycle parking at or near all stops and bicycle lanes on major roadways.

Noise: Stakeholders voiced concerns about noise from the operation of the LRT.

Vibration: Stakeholders voiced concerns about vibration during construction and operations.

Shortcutting and Parking in Neighborhoods: Stakeholders voiced concerns about people parking in residential neighborhoods to access the LRT or shortcutting through neighborhoods.

Larger or Additional Park 'N' Ride Locations: Larger or additional Park 'N' Ride locations are needed

Traffic Congestion at 178th Street and 87th Avenue: Suggest elevating tracks over intersection to minimize congestion.[14]

Funding Negotiations and the Public—OurLRT Coalition against P3s and #yeg4LRT

The south half of the Valley line alone will cost $1.8 billion dollars. While the City of Edmonton is providing $800 million, it required additional funding partners.[16]

In March 2013, the Federal Government of Canada announced P3 Canada Fund investment of up to $250-million in the southbound Mill Woods half of the Valley Line. This funding requires construction and operational management of the LRT line by a private contractor.[11] A coalition of Edmontonians formed to oppose this public–private partnership citing concerns about contract secrecy, erosion of public service delivery, and unionization impacts.[12] The City responded with a Frequently Asked Questions sheet on P3s intended to address and alleviate concerns.[13]

The city concurrently also began the #yeg4LRT campaign, not as a public-involvement initiative for project planning, but as an advocacy campaign to encourage Edmontonians to express support for LRT in order to encourage funding approval by federal and provincial governments. "During the first five days of the campaign, more than 1,000 people tweeted the hashtag #yeg4LRT. A video released on February 20, 2014 was viewed more than 3,000 times on YouTube and reached more than 7,000 users on Facebook."[16]

An important part of this phase of engagement began at the impetus of a private citizen seeking to help in a novel way with the use of social media. In the first week of March 2014, after the announcement of the Alberta provincial budget omitted any reference to funding for the south half of the Valley Line, a private individual, Dana DiTomaso, created a Twitter hashtag "SadDonIvenson" that acknowledged the disappointment

Figure 4.2 Sad Don Hashtag (DiTomaso 2014) [28]

in the Mayor's demeanor immediately following a key speech by the Premier of Alberta (see Figure 4.2).[28] Mayor Don Ivenson even entered the online conversation with a playful retweet (see Figure 4.3).[30] There soon followed 1000 re-Tweets and favorites associated with the hashtag,[27] and coverage of the trending social media story by the Huffington Post (a national online media website; Huffington Post 2014).[29] The impact of such an action is noted by the students of the second author of this case, who discussed this event in a course paper saying, "A simple response on Twitter appears to be a simple and quick act, but it speaks volumes to the users. When citizens feel that their thoughts are acknowledged, especially by a prominent figure such as the Mayor, it can result in a newfound level of loyalty and top of mind awareness. This level of engagement can result in a deeper level of citizen investment in the form of participation and discussion," Barry et al. (2014).[26]

Probably equally important, standard communications techniques were also used, including stories on traditional media and grass-roots efforts (letter writing and calls) directed to influence political officials involved, as well as meetings between the Mayor, the Alberta Finance Minister, and other cabinet ministers.

On March 11, about a week later, a commitment of $600 million in funding from the provincial government was announced ($400 million

I'm totally stress eating tonight. #ABbudget #saddoniveson #EatLocal

Figure 4.3 Mayor's Response (Iveson 2014)

in grants and a \$200-million interest-free loan to be repaid over 10 years; Kent 2014).[31] A further \$150 million of federal funding may be available through the Building Canada fund.[19]

Assessment and Learning

The project management of LRT expansion, even for just one half of one line, is extremely complicated and involves a huge stable of outside consultants and city staff. The task of successfully communicating public-involvement purposes and scope has been very large. The process was well-documented with dozens of key documents available online. A weakness of this documentation is that it was not archived in a user-friendly manner, as copies of public presentations are mixed with PI reports on the project pages, while other reports can only be found on the City Council SIRE archives. Inconsistent file naming practices makes it challenging for public users to find specific information or reassemble a timeline.

Based on review of reports, the process seems to be somewhat inconsistent in style and detail. While there is a wealth of evidence of consideration of and impacts from public feedback, there is also evidence that some Edmontonians felt frustrated that their ideas and concerns were not addressed. In those cases, blame was inevitably assigned to the consultation process. Some responses to these critiques in reports and media came across as dismissive (for example, listing the number of events held rather than addressing concerns about confusing consultations and reminding participants that they are not decision-makers).[2,20] There may also have been lack of clarity about the decision process for isolated elements (such as the decision to remove Edmonton's downtown footbridge). To some extent, however, claims of dismissiveness by the City or consultants or lack of clarity about the process inevitably occur from participants not satisfied with outcomes.

At the same time, there were numerous positive impacts of public engagement—with the number of positive outcomes rising as the project progressed. An important contributor to public buy-in appeared to consist of the process of solicitation from the public of names for the line (at low cost), and narrowing the over 3,000 names submitted to a shortlist of 5, for ultimate selection of the name, "Valley Line." Citizen input was also instrumental for selection of themes for stop/station elements, benches, and paving; choice of organic shaped canopies; confirming the importance of ease of access to businesses and community attractions, provision of bicycle parking and addressing other parking concerns, and further encouragement of Park "N" Ride usage.

An evaluation of the public-involvement process, as well as participant feedback on the process, was available in general PI Reports in accordance with the PIPs for the Concept and Design phases.[24,25] These reports contain much data but very little analysis on how to improve the PI process. They tend to be more of a compilation of information gathered. There is also heavy reliance on open house feedback forms as a measure of public opinion, and little integration of media and social media although both elements were planned for in the PIP. A process or rubric for weighing and analyzing these elements in order to assess the success of the PI process, note weaknesses, and suggest changes, would add practical value. The self-assessed score of "somewhat prepared" in the Design PIP Readiness Test indicates that there was room for improvement on this dimension. A consistent approach to reporting for each step across all public-involvement consultants could be helpful in tracking public involvement and developing clear expectations for the public.

The time span of this case, going back 40 years to 1977, but revived in earnest around 2009, vividly demonstrates the concepts of "hang time" and "churn" (discussed in Chapter 1 of this book). The projected budget alone for the Southeast Leg to Mill Woods has increased from $101 million in 1977 to $1.8 billion in 2014. The participants—citizens, political actors, administrators—were almost completely different from the onset. Neighborhoods and streets have been significantly updated. Public considerations, the green movement, energy costs, city extent, and transportation congestion, have all changed. But what did not happen to a large extent, as elsewhere, such as for the Walterdale Bridge, is decision lock-in and misaligned expectations. The project underwent a very effective "reset" around 2009, with detailed and thoughtful public engagement plans, that were largely carried out. And, if there was a challenge for public involvement, it may have simply been the enormous scope of the project and the volumes of data generated, calling attention to the need for synthesis and transparency for the various participants. A related opportunity arising from the extensive time span is the possibility of learning more about conducting effective public involvement over time.

Due to the size and cost of this project, public support was vital in securing funding from provincial and federal governments. This means that goodwill—or animosity—generated during the public-involvement process has a direct impact on the financial viability of expansive projects such as this. In particular, the advocacy elements of the #yeg4LRT campaign, the "#saddonivenson" thread of tweets and associated coverage, together with use of traditional media and a political "full court press" evidenced flashes of brilliance, and illustrates the importance of mobilizing public opinion for large projects such as this.

Overall, the LRT public-involvement effort merits a positive assessment, with occasional rough edges, but with evidence of increased expertise over time. This experience illustrates the need for a consistent and clearly synthesized engagement process for large projects, the relevance of hang time and participant churn, the need for securing provincial and federal funding for large projects (and the growing role of P3s), and

Figure 4.4 Mayor Don Iveson was joined in the groundbreaking ceremony by federal Minister of Infrastructure and Communities Amarjeet Sohi, Alberta Minister of Transportation and Minister of Infrastructure Brian Mason, and representatives from Edmonton's Indigenous communities, the Valley Line Citizen Working Groups and TransEd Partners.[15]

the emerging role of social media and opportunities for new styles of communications. Construction began on the southeast leg of the Valley Line with a groundbreaking ceremony (see Figure 4.4) on April 22, 2016.[15,17]

Sources

1. City of Edmonton 2008 LRT Expansion Public Survey Feedback May 2009.

2. *Edmonton Journal* April 12 2008 West LRT opposition heats up.

3. City of Edmonton Southeast Light Rail Transit Downtown to Mill Woods Corridor Selection Report March 2009.

4. City of Edmonton West and SE LRT Expansions Concept Public Involvement Plan March 2009.

5. City of Edmonton West and Southeast LRT Milestones Report April 2010.

6. City of Edmonton Southeast LRT Downtown to Millwoods Concept Plan Booklet April 2011.

7. City of Edmonton Southeast to West LRT: Preliminary Design Public Involvement Plan December 2011.

8. City of Edmonton Long-Term LRT Expansion LRT Network Plan March 2012, www.edmonton.ca/documents/PDF/Long_Term_LRT_Network_Plan_March_2012.pdf (accessed on October 1, 2016).

9. City of Edmonton Preliminary Design Process – Valley Line (SE to W LRT) April 2013, /www.edmonton.ca/documents/PDF/030413_Preliminary_Design_Process_SE_to_W_LRT.pdf (accessed on October 1, 2016).

10. *Edmonton Sun,* "Proposed Edmonton LRT bridge comes with a possible $65 million price tag," Angelique Rodrigues, February 6, 2013. www.edmontonsun.com/2013/02/06/proposed-edmonton-lrt-bridge-comes-with-a-possible-65-million-price-tag (accessed on October 1, 2016).

11. Government of Canada and City of Edmonton Announce Public-Private Partnership (P3) to Speed up Light Rail Transit Access for Edmontonians March 2013

12. http://blogs.edmontonjournal.com/2013/09/12/coalition-fighting-p3-planned-for-southeast-edmonton-lrt/ (accessed in April 2014).

13. City of Edmonton P3 Factsheet September 2013.

14. City of Edmonton Valley Line LRT Final Preliminary Design November 2013

15. City of Edmonton Valley Line Project History, https://www.edmonton.ca/projects_plans/valley_line_lrt/concept-planning-project-history.aspx (accessed on October 1, 2016).

16. City of Edmonton YEG 4 LRT public advocacy campaign http://www.4lrt.com/ (accessed in April 2014).

17. City of Edmonton Valley Line (SE to West LRT): Mill Woods to Lewis Farms, webpage, www.edmonton.ca/projects_plans/valley-line-lrt-mill-woods-to-lewis-farms.aspx (accessed October 1, 2016).

18. *Edmonton Journal,* January 31 2013 City names LRT lines, grumbling follows.

19. *Edmonton Journal,* March 11, 2014 Edmonton's Southeast LRT on track after province promises to fill $600 million funding gap.

20. *Edmonton Journal*, March 19, 2014 Edmonton LRT-expansion critics call for more transparency http://www.edmontonsun.com/2014/03/19/edmonton-lrt-expansion-critics-call-for-more-transparency (accessed in April 2014).

21. City of Edmonton LRT Route Planning & Evaluation Criteria March 2012.

22. City of Edmonton Public Engagement Process Preliminary Design Stage 4 – Refinement Report July 2013.

23. City of Edmonton Report West Light Rail Transit Downtown to Lewis Estates, October 2009; https://www.edmonton.ca/documents/PDF/2009_West_LRT_Corridor.pdf (accessed on October 1, 2016).

24. City of Edmonton. Comment Form Results – West LRT, November 2010.

25. Comment Form Results – South-East LRT, November 2010.

26. Barry, Bianca; Victor Chiu; Allison Leonard; David Manuntag; Shuai Ouyang; Danial Roth; Lowell Tautchin (2014), "Edmonton Online: Assessing the State of Municipal Online Media," Term Paper for course BUS 480-X50, University of Alberta School of Business (Jan–April, 2014).

27. Dahlen, Jenn. (2014, April 3). Jenn Dahlen Tweet. Retrieved April 2014, from Twitter.com/jenndahl: https://twitter.com/jenndahl/status/451739472556597248

28. DiTomaso, D. (2014, March 6). Dana DiTomaso Tweet. Retrieved April 2014, from Twitter.com/danaditomaso: https://twitter.com/danaditomaso/status/441726080840253440.

29. Huffington Post. (2014, March 7). Sad Don Iveson, Edmonton Mayor, Becomes Awesome Meme. Retrieved April 2014, from Huffington Post: http://www.huffingtonpost.ca/2014/03/07/sad-don-iveson-edmonton_n_4921116.html

30. Iveson, D. (2014, March 6). Don Iveson Tweet. Retrieved April 2014, from Twitter.com/doniveson: https://twitter.com/doniveson/status/441800325901471745/photo/1.

31. Kent, Gordon (1014), "It's a go! $600-million boost from province puts southeast LRT from Mell Woods on track," *Edmonton Journal*, pp. 1 & 4, March 12, 2014.

CHAPTER 5

Converting to a Freeway

The Interchange at 149th and Yellowhead Trail

Heather Stewart and Paul R. Messinger

In 2012, the Transportation Services Department conducted public-involvement planning and implementation for an interchange at 149th Street and Yellowhead Trail (see Figure 5.1). This project included early and open-ended public-involvement activities in an attempt to help avoid confusion and conflict around decision-making factors which had been a challenge in some previous major projects.

Figure 5.1 Preferred strategy: One-way service roads

Context and Catalyst

The 149th Street Interchange at Yellowhead Trail project was part of an early phase of a long-term Yellowhead Trail Strategic Plan to develop the Yellowhead Trail into a freeway, which requires converting intersections into interchanges.

Planning

A typical public-involvement plan (PIP) starts with technical analysis and the drafting of a proposed concept plan for the project, which is presented at a public open house for feedback, adjusted in response to feedback, and presented at one or more cycles of further open houses to reach the Recommended Plan. This type of standard PIP focuses on the foundation level of the city of Edmonton's Public Involvement continuum, "sharing information to build awareness." The 149th Street project included Information Sharing as well as the next level in the continuum, Consultation ("Testing ideas or concepts to build knowledge" and "Collaborating to build commitment"). The most engaged level of public involvement, Active Participation ("Sharing decision-making" and "Delegating decision-making") was not attempted for this project.(See p. 38 for the Public Involvement Continuum.)

Instead of starting with a proposed concept plan for an interchange and then running public-involvement activities to adjust that plan, the 149th Street project planned to collect public-involvement feedback first. Public-involvement activities were conducted alongside technical analysis as part of research study process in 2012 which informed the concept plan development in 2013.

Engagement

Public-involvement activities included open houses, and targeted interviews, and stakeholder input groups (SIGs). Open houses are typically advertised by a variety of means including roadside signs, but traditional printed roadside signs are banned on high speed roadways like Yellowhead Trail, so the project team successfully pioneered the use of existing electronic billboards to promote the open houses. Open houses and targeted interviews with business and community stakeholders provided information and collected feedback but also served as points of recruitment for a SIG of around 14 members. The SIG was assembled in summer 2012 and participated in a series of five workshops where key planning factors and options were explained, discussed, and evaluated. SIG feedback became a central element of the second Open House in which possible concept plan options were presented. The feedback was compiled and one final Recommended Option was presented to the community in early 2013.

Impact

The Recommended Option that resulted from this process suggests that public-involvement feedback did have an effect on project planning in this model. The assumption from the City of Edmonton throughout the project was that the solution would be a type of interchange, as reflected in the project title: "149th Street Interchange at Yellowhead Trail." However after work-shopping various options with the SIG, the final conclusion was that the best solution (to balance community and business impacts with the need to make the Yellowhead Trail a free flow transportation corridor) was not in interchange. Instead a "right-in, right-out" style of intersection was selected as the final recommendation. This option allows access on and off of the Yellowhead from the right lanes but prevents crossing from one side of the Yellowhead to the other via 149th Street. This "right-in, right-out" model would cost approximately $200 million, versus approximately $400 million for a full freeway interchange.

Assessment and Learning

The project is currently in the final stages of technical concept planning and costing in the Facility and Capital Planning section. Interview feedback suggests that the process was labor-intensive but proceeded well.

Two distinctive features characterized the public-involvement process. (1) Public-involvement feedback to particular alternatives was collected as an input to and alongside concept planning. (2) SIGs were used, together with open houses, targeted interviews, and Internet questionnaires. While public involvement using all these features would only be considered in the future for the most sensitive and complex projects, the Facility and Capital Planning section is continuing to test the concept of gathering primary feedback prior to developing an initial concept plan for presentation at a public Open House. Internet questionnaires were also quite helpful, and similar rapid online feedback tools will likely be used to inform early concept plan design in the future.

Sources

Compiled from CPI interview research responses and the Transportation Service Department's Public Involvement Plan (PIP).

CHAPTER 6

Too Late to Streetscape 99th

Heather Stewart and Paul R. Messinger

"99th Street Is Open Again: Celebrate! Mourn!"
—Todd Babiak, *Edmonton Journal* (2011)[1]

Context and Catalyst

The Scona Road Widening and 99th Street Rehabilitation project of Spring 2011 to Spring 2013 was planned as a rehabilitation activity only. For this type of rehabilitation project, where no substantive changes are being made, the planning assessment does not call for a public-involvement plan (PIP). The key outreach activity for rehabilitation is to inform the public of the project timeline, any road closures, and traffic disruptions that are required for the project to move forward. This was accomplished in a public meeting in January 2011. According to an *Edmonton Journal* blog, the limitations of the project scope for 99th Street caught Rob McDonald, then president of the Old Strathcona Community League, off guard.

"There was no opportunity for changes," McDonald said. "They said it was already too late. The 'consultation' was simply an information session."[1]

Scona Road Widening and Landscaping work was proceeding at the same time, and had undergone public-involvement processes although there were community demands to change the approved plan during the construction stage, which could not be accommodated. This may have contributed to frustration around the 99th Street Rehabilitation project.

Planning and Engagement

Most of the rehabilitation work was repaving, resurfacing, streetlight and utility upgrades, and miscellaneous repairs. As the work was underway, residents began to express concern about the traffic levels on 99th Street. The community league got involved and connected with the local councilor to try to augment the plan. An impromptu community meeting was called with Transportation staff, the City Councilor for Ward 8, Community League President and other executives, and residents. This was not a standard preplanned and publicly documented public-involvement activity, but it was accepted as a "public involvement procedure" by Transportation staff.[2] As reported the local newspaper, city representatives cited road standards that precluded a more involved streetscaping project:

> "We have to follow national design guidelines from the Transportation Association of Canada," said Brian Latte, from the city transportation department. "As the speed of the road increases, you want to move fixed objects as far from the road as possible. What we have here is a road allowance that was designed in the early 1900s. Space is tight. It's not practical to remove a lane, and purchasing property to allow more room for sidewalks wasn't an option."[1]

During the public meeting, Ward 8 Councilor supported the community demands that the City conduct streetscaping and dedicated funds toward that.

> It's too bad about 99th Street, but I don't think we'll ever see this happen again," he said. "These guidelines aren't standards, and I think they're antiquated. They're about cars, and in many ways they clash with the pedestrian realm. It does bring up larger questions that need to be asked about how we can do this sort of work, yet still have a walkable city.[1]

This late-stage addition of screetscaping presented some technical challenges to the project as the structural work had already been completed. According to a City transportation professional:

> Because it was done after we had already built what was there it led to a lot of limitations as to what we could do. Ideally, what we could do is if he tells us for example to put trees in we'd be able to put in the tree grades and the sidewalk and make the trees work in the sidewalk, but because we had just replaced the sidewalk we couldn't rip off existing sidewalk, so we could only plant trees beside the sidewalk. But there was no land, so we had to get agreements on private property to put the trees, so it wasn't as beneficial as it could have been for the city, it wasn't the best way to do it, but it was something that was kind of forced. It wasn't the best way to do it, we could have done it better if the decision had been made beforehand.[3]

The Streetscape project was led by another Department, the Office of Great Neighborhoods.

Impact, Assessment, and Learning

Ultimately the outcome on 99th Street satisfied no one. Several issues were raised: delays between long-term planning and project implementation which led to residents feeling out-of-the-loop, inconsistencies with city and neighborhood goals, technical design standards that may be driver-centric, challenges in managing resident expectations of what projects and public information sessions are expected to achieve, and, finally, the potential for inconsistencies in what various neighborhood resident associations and councilors are able to negotiate for their communities given limits on resources and advocacy capacity.

Given the challenges raised by this project, it is unfortunate that a version of a standard PIP, report, or evaluation was not developed, even retroactively, in order to assess the situation and learn from it further.

Sources

1. Babiak, Todd (2011) "99th Street Is Open Again: Celebrate! Mourn!" *Edmonton Journal Blog* (October 24, 2011), http://blogs.edmontonjournal.com/2011/10/24/99th-street-is-open-again-celebrate-mourn/ (Accessed in October 1, 2016).

2. City of Edmonton – Scona Road Widening and 99 Street Rehabilitation Webpage, http://www.edmonton.ca/transportation/road_projects/scona-road-widening-and-99-street-rehabilitation.aspx (Accessed in April 2014).

3. CPI Research Interview Transcript 2014.

CHAPTER 7

Public Pushback on Bicycle Routes

Moein Khanlari and Paul R. Messinger

Edmonton's Bicycle route implementation plan has been moving forward since 2010. Despite overall success in adding more bike routes each year, the project has faced public dissatisfaction in some neighborhoods. This discontentment has led the City to revisit its public consultation efforts in a way that allows public input to modify previously determined parameters of the projects such as the location of bike routes and route selection criteria. The changes are expected to ensure that citizens play a more central role in the development of the City's bike routes.

Context and Catalyst

Edmonton's Bicycle Transportation Plan (BTP) was updated and approved in 2009 and lays out the City's strategy over the next ten years for transforming Edmonton into a bicycle-friendly city.[1] This strategic plan is part of the implementation steps for Edmonton's Transportation Master Plan (The Way We Move).[i,3] Edmonton's bicycle network is envisioned as a two-level

---

[i] www.edmonton.ca/transportation/cycling_walking/bicycle-transportation-plan.aspx (accessed on October 1, 2016).

system comprised of a city-wide network that forms the 'skeleton' and a connector system that creates links within the neighborhoods.[ii] The plan will eventually add 489 km of new bicycle paths to the city in three phases.

Phase I of the project, planned for the 2009 to 2013 period, includes the preparation of bikeways that did not involve major costs or upgrades and could be implemented by paint demarcation and adding signage along the routes. This phase aimed to produce visible near-term results with the addition of 125 km of city-wide and 77 km of connector network bikeways with an estimated cost of $34,300,000.

Phase II involves bikeways with moderate-to-major expenditures and includes 145 and 90 km of city-wide and connector networks while phase III deals with bikeways that face major constraints and require regional planning.

Phase III covers 52 km of city-wide bikeways. The Bicycle Network Plan Map lays out the conceptual plan for the different components of this bicycle network, and is accompanied by the Bicycle Network Priority Map as its implementation plan. Appendix 2 shows the progress of phase I up to May 2013.

Planning

Prior to April 2014, the City of Edmonton's website used to include the following statement regarding public involvement on bike routes:

> Public involvement is an important part of designing on-street bike infrastructure. When an on-street bike route is being planned and designed, consultation is held to get input on the unique characteristics of the street where it will be located, including how vehicles and pedestrians use the street and how the route connects to the neighbourhood activity centres.

This statement captured the City's focus at that time on collecting public input only on the details of a preplanned bike route rather than involving the public in major route decisions.

[ii] http://www.edmonton.ca/transportation/BicycleTransportationPlanSummary Report.pdf (accessed on May 30, 2014).

Two separate rounds of public consultations were conducted for the 2012 and 2013 planned bike routes. In this case study, we will focus on the 2013 bike routes public-involvement initiative.[2]

The 2013 bike routes consultation project ran from January to April 2013 and sought citizen feedback to identify unforeseen issues or unique uses of roadways/shared use paths to inform the design of nine bike routes in 2013. The formal scope of this public-involvement effort did not allow for any changes to the bike routes as these were presumed to have been approved with the 2009 BTP.

Directly affected stakeholders[iii] were invited to smaller stakeholder meetings, and the general public was engaged through open houses and an online survey. The communication for the project was carried out via outdoor signs, print advertising, flyers, community league/club/ group activations, and the City's website as well as the Twitter account #yegbikes.

The following indicators of success for the public-involvement process were identified in the planning stage: [iv, 2]

- Turnout at meetings/use of online survey/social media feedback (Expectations: 50 percent response rate for invitations to stakeholder meetings, and an average of 25 feedback comments per open house meeting).
- Quality information for planners collected from meetings.
- Balanced media coverage that reflects the City's efforts to inform and consult with the public.
- Major concerns with the 2013 bike routes identified before the implementation phase.
- Few to no instances of residents saying they were not aware of the bike routes at implementation.

In addition, feedback collected from participants and online surveys was used to evaluate the public-involvement process.

[iii] Senior center administrators, large apartment and complex managers, business owners, church leaders, community league leaders, school board leaders, City Councilors, facility managers, cycling club representatives.

[iv] 2013 bike routes consultation report.

Engagement

In total, fourteen stakeholder meetings were conducted consisting of 20-minute presentations by City staff followed by invitations to participants to ask questions or share their concerns and suggestions with City representatives.

Major stakeholders as well as residents adjacent to the routes also received invitations via mail to participate in three public open houses. Participants could drop in over a three-hour time period to view design plans and talk to City representatives. In the third open house event, that is, the preconstruction open house, received feedback, and final decisions were reported back to participants.

The above activities produced a total of 2,004 instances of interactions comprised of meeting attendance, comments, and survey responses.

Impact

The public-involvement report for this project documents several comments received from citizens on each of the nine routes. The project report clearly identifies the eventual list of public demands that could be met and describes their impact on the design decisions.

In addition, a number of overall themes and concerns were derived from public input which is included in Appendix 1 to this report. Most of these themes could not be directly addressed because the plan was already fixed or because participant concerns fell outside the parameters set for this consultation process.

Participant feedback on evaluation surveys showed general satisfaction with the details of the current public-involvement initiative, but also contained indications that citizens were not as satisfied with the city's overall efforts to involve them in bike route decisions. In the final preconstruction open house, 69 participants returned 28 evaluation forms. These evaluations indicated that, despite relatively general satisfaction with the details of the public-involvement activity, such as its usefulness and informativeness, there was a significant division of opinion on satisfaction with the 'City's efforts to consider public input for the on-street bike routes'.[v]

[v] Eleven people were satisfied/strongly satisfied while twelve others were dissatisfied/strongly dissatisfied and five participants were neutral.

Assessment and Learning

The public-involvement project for the bike routes made considerable effort to reflect citizen views in design considerations. The implementation of bikeways in several neighborhoods has been uneventful which might be a sign of general satisfaction with the project's outcome. However, despite the fact that this public-involvement project was carried out meticulously, some inherent restrictions limited its impact. The main limitation of this public-involvement effort was its scope, which left no leeway for reconsidering the location of the bike routes. This shortcoming is partly reflected in some participants' dissatisfaction with the City's efforts to involve the public. Explicit controversy, however, started with the implementation plan.

Implementation of the bike lanes in several neighborhoods was met with objections from both motorists and cyclists. Motorists expressed frustration and confusion with the implemented changes to the roads, and cyclists' expressed concerns regarding their safety. The extent of concerns attracted the attention of the media and City officials as people started questioning the usefulness of some of the implemented bike lanes. Citizens felt that they were not adequately consulted in bike route decisions and actively pursued alternative solutions. Edmonton's Ward 10 is an example of a neighborhood that requested major changes to the implemented bike routes.

Implementation of the BTP mainly started in the south side of Edmonton, which includes much of Ward 10. Public feedback from the communities in this area regarding traffic congestion and safety, among other things, led their Councilor, Michael Walters, to systematically collect public input and prepare a report for the Council on the affected communities' views regarding the implemented bike lanes.[vi] Many Citizens expressed concerns regarding the bike lanes on 106 Street south of 51 Avenue and 40 Avenue from 119 Street to 106 Street

Councilor Walters said in an interview:

> We have put bike lanes in communities that were not prepared for them. What we've done in older neighborhoods is, kind of, jammed them into existing commuter roads without proper education and people are not using them . . . based on the research

---

[vi] Ward 10 bike lanes report, by Councilor Michael Walters.

that we've done, . . . the bikeways that we've installed aren't going to increase ridership . . .What I'm going to ask administration is to give us alternative routes . . . that maintain connectivity of the whole network but actually relocate the lanes installed in ward 10 to places that the community will actually buy into . . . that will increase ridership among the residents of my ward.

As a result of the recent public dissatisfaction, the City has postponed the installation of more bike lanes on some routes to revisit its public-involvement efforts for bike routes. The City has refocused its efforts by committing to engage citizens in decisions regarding where the bike routes should be located in addition to more cosmetic details. The City's new campaign, called 'What the B*ke' has just started and has already elicited a great amount of online feedback.[vii] In addition to suggesting routes, citizens can also help to determine the criteria that City decision-makers will use to choose from the existing alternatives.[viii,4]

Edmonton's Bike Plan is in the early stages of its implementation and the initial feedback from citizens indicates that they demand to have a say on more than just cosmetic details of preplanned bike routes. The City has responded by honoring these demands with the hope of realigning the implementation of the bike plan with citizen expectations.[ix] New consultation efforts will help the City to better understand the range of opinions regarding bike lanes and ensure a smooth transition of Edmonton to becoming a bicycle-friendly city.

Sources

1. [The City of Edmonton] 2009 Bicycle Transportation Plan www. edmonton.ca/transportation/PDF/BicycleTransportationPlanSummaryReport.pdf (accessed October 1, 2016).

[vii] http://engagingedmonton.ca/portals/150/1533 (accessed on May 30, 2014).

[viii] http://www.cbc.ca/news/canada/edmonton/city-council-asks-for-public-s-help-designing-new-bike-lanes-1.2647991 (accessed on October 1, 2016).

[ix] http://www.edmontonjournal.com/news/insight/bike-lanes/index.html (accessed on May 30, 2014).

2. [The City of Edmonton] 2013 Bicycle Route Design Public Consultation, What We Heard: Stakeholder Feedback, Final Interim Report (not
   publicly available). A publicly available summary is www.edmonton.ca
   /documents/PDF/Bikes2013_FactSheet_WWH_April17.pdf (accessed
   October 1, 2016).
3. Websites associated with the City of Edmonton (www.edmonton
   .ca & www.engagingedmonton.ca).
4. Referenced media reports.

APPENDIX 1

Major themes derived from public input in the 2013 Bike Routes Consultation project

- Some embraced the addition of new facilities that would encourage cycling, connect more routes, and result in a healthier city, while others felt the city should focus investment on maintaining existing road infrastructure before investing in cycling infrastructure.
- Some felt the cycling routes would inconvenience drivers by slowing down traffic and congesting streets, while others felt bike routes would have a traffic-calming affect that would benefit local residents.
- Some felt the addition of the lanes would encourage cycling by giving people a dedicated space to cycle along the roadways that reach major destinations. Others expressed concern that the roads were too congested to offer a safe place for cyclists and suggested cycling routes should be located off-road or on quiet residential roads. Concerns were also raised about safety for children and cyclists on proposed routes near school drop-off zones.
- In areas where on-street parking could not be maintained with the addition of bike infrastructure, many residents, businesses, and churches noted concerns about the impact this change would have on their guests, family members and patrons. Some suggested these changes could not be accepted, and others noted different options needed to be pursued to add parking to side streets or to lift parking limitations during designated hours.

- Many noted a need to ensure snow is removed from the new cycling lanes in the winter, while others suggested the cost of removing snow from these lanes would be potentially prohibitive.
- Many feel education about how to use the bike routes and enforcing bylaws is necessary to ensure cyclists, motorists, and pedestrians are able to move safely.
- Many expressed concerns that the consultation process was not aligned to discuss options or changes to the route locations.

APPENDIX 2

The implemented and delayed bike route projects (Up-to-date in May 2014)

2013 Delayed Bike Route Projects

- 76 Avenue from 78 Street to 100 Street, 100 Street from 76 Avenue to Saskatchewan Drive – On hold
- 132 Avenue from 82 Street to 91 Street – On hold

2013 Completed Bike Route Projects

- **95 Avenue** – 145 Street to 189 Street
- **81 Street** – 119 Avenue to Yellowhead Trail, 119 Avenue – 76 Street to 82 Street, 78 Avenue – 117 Avenue to 82 Street
- **97 Street** – 63 Avenue to 82 Avenue
- **106 Street** – 34 Avenue to 51 Avenue, 40 Avenue – 106 to 119 Street
- **114 Street** – 34 Avenue to 44a Avenue, 115 Street – 46 to 60 Avenue
- **116 Street** – 71 Avenue to 73 Avenue, 73 Avenue – 115 Street to 116 Street, 115 Street – 73 Avenue to University Avenue
- **Saddleback Road** – routes connecting to Blue Quill Park

2012 Completed Bike Route Projects

- **116 Street** – 87 Avenue to Saskatchewan Dr
- **121 Street** – 100 Avenue to 106 Avenue

- **189 Street** – 87 Avenue to 95 Avenue
- **82 Street** – 127 Avenue to 137 Avenue
- **Leger Road** – 23 Avenue to Leger Way
- **Wolf Willow Road** – East of 170 Street

2012 Delayed Bike Route Projects

- **121 Avenue** – 34 Street to 69 Street
- **Abbottsfield** – Victoria Trail to 34 Street

2011 Completed Bike Route Projects

- **97 Street** – 34 Avenue to 83 Avenue
- **106 Street** – 51 Avenue to Saskatchewan Dr
- **Saddleback Road** – a loop around the communities of Skyrattler, Keheewin, and Ermineskin
- **69 Avenue** – 170 Street to 178 Street
- **76 Avenue** – Gateway Blvd to Saskatchewan Dr
- **40 Street** – Hermitage Rd to Clareview LRT Station

2010 Completed Bike Route Projects

- Mill Woods Road Loop

CHAPTER 8

Complete Streets

Learning from Past Pushback

Moein Khanlari and Paul R. Messinger

The City of Edmonton developed a Complete Streets policy to be used in planning, design, and construction of new or existing streets in order to ensure efficient and convenient access for all street users.[2] The policy was developed in consultation with internal and external stakeholders through workshops and an online discussion forum. The policy was approved by Edmonton's City Council in May 2013.[3]

Context and Catalyst

A Complete Street is a street whose design takes into account its surrounding area context and land use to eventually enable its users to safely move along or across it regardless of their ages, abilities, and transportation modes. The desirable Complete Street has a maximum diversity of user types and transportation modes, accomodating the safe and efficient movement of cyclists, pedestrians, transit users, motorists, buses, and trucks. The ambitious idea of transforming city streets to Complete Streets is being pursued in several major Canadian cities and there are several implemented examples.[i] This policy was developed subsequent to, and probably in reaction to, negative public sentiment from the 99th Street Rehabilitation case and the Bicycle Routes case.

---

[i] http://completestreetsforcanada.ca/map (accessed October 1, 2016).

Figure 8.1 A multi-mode complete street[1]

Edmonton's Complete Streets project was developed to provide guidance for the implementation of Edmonton's Transportation Master Plan (The Way We Move). This policy will affect the planning, design, and construction of new streets or the rehabilitation of existing ones. Edmonton is the fourth city in Canada to adopt such a policy with Calgary being the first.

Planning

The public-involvement process for this project was conducted over a period of one year through a number of workshops with internal and external stakeholders and elicitation of feedback from the general public through an online forum.

Engagement

The workshops and the online forum mainly focused on informing citizens and receiving feedback on draft guidelines. The online forum consisted of two phases.[ii] In phase I, general feedback was sought on different topics, whereas phase II mostly focused on getting feedback on the prepared Complete streets guidelines draft. Phase I elicited approximately

[ii] http://completestreets.dialogue-app.com/phase1 (accessed April 1, 2014). See http://www.delib.net/resources/Edmonton_Complete_Streets_Case_Study.pdf (accessed October 1, 2016).

172 comments. Citizens were able to post their ideas anonymously, but they had to log in to be able to comment on existing posts. Assuming that each of 66 anonymous users who initiated a discussion was a unique visitor, 100 unique individuals participated in phase I of the online forum.[iii] The top five most active participants left 17, 14, 10, 6, and 5 comments. Phase II elicited approximately 61 comments by 15 unique participants.[iv]

Impact

The input received from citizens was used in the development of the Complete Streets policy. However, the actual impact of citizens' input and their contributions to the policy has not been demonstrated after the project's completion. While demonstration of public impact on decisions is challenging, it could encourage further participation of citizens in decisions that affect them.

Assessment and Learning

The use of an online forum for eliciting public input made the project more available to the general public. Many ideas were put forward by the forum participants and some discussion took place among a few active participants. Discussion of ideas can shed light on their strengths and weaknesses which can provide grounds for a more careful consideration of the ideas that survive such initial examination. Online participation tools can benefit from adding small tweaks and incentives that encourage conversation among participants. This project collected input from citizens and incorporated it in the development of the Complete Streets guidelines.

Despite the existing challenges of demonstrating the impact of citizen input on decision outcomes, creating transparency on how public input maps onto decisions can nurture citizen trust and encourage higher levels

---

[iii] Five comments were received via email and posted on the forum by project staff members.

[iv] Of these, 33 comments came from one user ID. One interesting comment suggested the adoption of a competing strategy, called 'Pedestrians First', which puts priority on pedestrians.

of participation. A simple way of achieving this purpose would be to develop an *impact tree* that takes the received comments and links them to overarching themes which are then linked to the decision outcomes in a tree structure. Such a structure could also identify any public input that was not ultimately used in decision-making, hence allowing decision-makers to easily focus attention on ideas that were not previously used and reassess their relevance, if necessary. To even make the process more transparent to the citizens, the rationale for the adoption of some ideas and dismissal of others could be provided. Making the input-to-outcome path more transparent would allow citizens to see that they were heard, and better exhibit the effort that goes into involving the public.

Sources

1. http://www.edmonton.ca/city_government/city_vision_and_strategic_plan/complete-streets.aspx (accessed October 1, 2016).

2. https://www.edmonton.ca/city_government/documents/Roads Traffic/Edmonton-Complete-Streets-Guidelines_05062013.pdf (accessed October 1, 2016).

3. www.edmonton.ca/city_government/city_vision_and_strategic_plan/complete-streets-history.aspx (accessed October 1, 2016).

CHAPTER 9

The Goods Movement Strategy

Engaging Multiple Stakeholders

Moein Khanlari and Paul R. Messinger

The Goods Movement Strategy project was initiated in 2012 in response to a need for up-to-date information on goods movement patterns and trucking industry needs. The project involved collecting data on truck movement and feedback from relevant stakeholders on their needs and concerns. (A representative example of daily truck trip patterns in Edmonton is shown in Figure 9.1.) The collected input was used to develop a Goods Movement Strategy that appeared before the City Council in Spring 2014 for approval. The project used a combination of methods to collect input from a diverse group of stakeholders to develop the strategy. The project enjoyed a well-planned public-involvement process with important and uncontroversial planning and policy outcomes.

Context and Catalyst

Edmonton is one of Canada's fastest growing cities and is projected to experience substantial economic growth over the next decade. Edmonton's Transportation Master Plan, The Way We Move, highlights the City's commitment to efficient and safe commercial transportation as part of the infrastructure needed to support this economic growth.[1] Since the

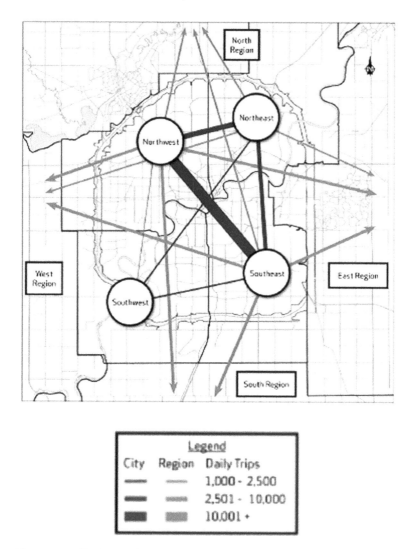

Figure 9.1 Daily truck trip patterns

transportation of goods and services throughout the city of Edmonton and its surrounding region is largely carried out by trucks, the City was interested in understanding truck movement patterns in order to enhance the efficient movement of goods in the City.

In 2012, the information available on truck movement within Edmonton was limited to the findings of a 1997 City-Wide Truck Route study and a 2001 Commodity Flow Study. On April 10, 2012, City councilors raised questions at the Transportation and Infrastructure Committee meeting that led to passing a motion to update the 1997 Truck Route study.

The study aimed to help the City better understand the changes in truck movement patterns over the previous decade and answer questions regarding the impact of the light rail transit (LRT) and the Anthony Henday Drive expansion on truck movements, the impact of adding or removing truck routes on the trucking industry, changes in truck volume, types of load and commodity flows, and proportion of internal versus externally destined trips, among other things. In addition, the City was interested in better understanding the needs and concerns of the trucking industry and truckers regarding goods movement. Consequently, a project was undertaken to collect up-to-date data and develop a goods movement strategy for the City of Edmonton that reflected relevant stakeholders' needs and supported the implementation of the City's Transportation Master Plan.

Planning

The public consultation for this project was carried out over a 15-month period from September 2012 to November 2013. The Public-Involvement Plan (PIP) for this project was developed by the City's Transportation Planning Branch together with an external consultant.[2] The project had a well-developed PIP that outlined the reasons and methods of involving the public, the type of information being sought, decision-makers, potential stakeholders, the public input integration process, and a public-involvement evaluation process. An important dimension built into the plan was to request direct feedback from participating stakeholders on each draft of the strategy which allowed participants to ensure their input had been factored in the development of the strategic objectives and actions.

Identified stakeholders included internal stakeholders from the City (Transportation Planning, Transportation Operations, Sustainable Development, Edmonton Economic Development Corporation), government and industry representatives,[i] external stakeholders,[ii] truckers, and trucking companies. The Capital Region board, the general trucker community, and the general public were also included as potential stakeholders mainly for information sharing purposes. A useful tactic for identifying other potential stakeholders was to ask identified stakeholders to recommend additional people and entities that needed to be consulted.

Engagement

Several techniques were employed to involve the public including 31 one-on-one scoping interviews with representatives from different stakeholder groups, roadside truck surveys (conducted from Sep. to Oct. 2012), 11 truck ride-alongs (May 2013), an industry consultation workshop (April 10, 2013), a community consultation workshop (May 2, 2013), a combined community-industry workshop (June 10, 2013), a public open house (November 20, 2013), and online surveys for feedback on draft strategic goals and the final draft of the strategy document. The open house was held at the conclusion of the project to present the Final Draft of the Goods Movement Strategy and receive input before its presentation to the City Council.[4]

The roadside truck surveys were collected from 2,294 drivers of trucks with a gross vehicle weight of 4,500 kg or more at 14 different locations around the city over 14 days. Tuesday through Friday between 9 a.m. and 3 p.m. were chosen as data collection times due to higher truck volumes during these off-peak periods. The findings of this study are reported in the 2013 Roadside Truck Survey report and were used in the development of the Goods Movement Strategy.[4]

---

[i] Chamber of Commerce, Edmonton Economic Development Corporation, Port Alberta, Edmonton International Airport, CN Rail, CP Rail, Alberta Motor Transport Association, Northeast Capital Industrial Association (Industrial Heartland), Chemistry Industry Association of Canada (Regional office in Ardrossan), Alberta Sand and Gravel Association, Leduc-Nisku Economic Development Authority, Alberta Food Processors Association, Acheson Business Association.

[ii] Transport Canada, Edmonton Police Service, RCMP, Air Canada, WestJet, First Air, University of Alberta, Alberta Medical Officer of Health.

Thirty-one, fourteen, and nineteen industry and community organizations were respectively represented in the first, second, and third workshops. Following the workshops, a draft of the prepared strategic objectives and actions was made available on the City of Edmonton website for all stakeholders and the general public. Visitors were able to submit their feedback through an online survey tool. Following the third workshop, the strategy document was again refined, finalized, and made available online from July to September 2013 for review and feedback. In total, 110 people took the online survey on the final draft of the document. The majority of respondents (about 80 percent) to the online survey on the final version of the goods movement strategy guidelines had not participated in any of the consultation activities. The overall average rating for the effectiveness of the strategic objectives was 3.7 out of 5, and 69 percent of the respondents felt it was important or very important that the strategy be implemented.

An open house event was planned to conclude the PI process and was advertised in three Edmonton papers and the City's Facebook and Twitter pages in addition to emails sent to communications departments of several relevant organizations and a public service announcement that was sent to media. Despite all these communications, only thirteen people attended the open house event, and five comment forms were submitted. This outcome suggests that open houses may not be suitable in projects which are not immediately relevant to the general public.

Impact

Stakeholder comments throughout the project were collected and summarized by the external consultant. Public input was effectively used through an iterative process in the development of strategies, priorities, and associated objectives and actions. First, a set of Goods Movement principles was developed based on the initial information collected from stakeholders. Subsequent feedback through workshops and postworkshop online surveys was used to further develop and finalize the Goods Movement Strategy draft. Participants also provided valuable information regarding specific locations and priorities for improvement. These more specific chunks of public input were summarized in an appendix to the

Goods Movement Strategy document called the Implementation Plan.[2] Overall, public input was effectively utilized for the development of the final draft of the Goods Movement strategy. Due to the nature of this project, which involved the development of strategies, and the iterative process used to arrive at the strategies and their associated objectives and actions, the impact of public input on project outcomes is easy to observe and potentially measure.

The final outcome, as noted on the City website was that "The Edmonton Goods Movement Strategy was presented to City Council's Transportation Committee meeting on June 18, 2014 along with the Goods Movement Policy. The Policy was adopted by City Council on June 25, 2014. The purpose of the policy is to guide transportation, funding and land use decisions to enhance the efficiency and safety of goods movement in the City of Edmonton within a regional context."[5]

Assessment and Learning

The PIP for this project identifies the main indicators of success for the public-involvement process as (1) involving the appropriate industry and government stakeholder groups through interviews and workshops (i.e., the representativeness criterion) and (2) extracting actionable input with positive contribution toward the development of Goods Movement strategies. The project succeeded in bringing in major relevant stakeholders and promoting the identification and participation of other potential stakeholders. Indeed, the "snowball" method of asking stakeholders to suggest additional relevant stakeholders is exemplary; and this approach should be carried over to other similar forms of public involvement. The use of multiple procedures to elicit stakeholder views ensured that the diverse interests of the stakeholders were reflected in the received input. The multiple tools used were exemplary. Finally, the consideration of policy makers of public-involvement input at each stage of the process, and the frequent updates to stakeholders along the way, led to incorporation of public input into policy. Overall, public-involvement effort was conducted and integrated into policy very effectively.

Some relatively minor areas for improvement consist of the following. Although, the public-involvement report mentions the polarization of views regarding issues such as the use of 75th Street as a truck route, it does not address the extent of such conflicts, how they were handled, and whether they were resolved. It would be beneficial to document such conflicts and decision-makers' responses to them in public-involvement reports, as these conflicts are likely to resurface in future if they are not recognized and officially addressed. In addition, the PIP for the project indicated that the information from participants in interviews and stakeholder workshops as well as participants' responses to an online process evaluation survey would be used to evaluate the public-involvement process. The public-involvement report does not clarify how this information was used for evaluation purposes, which suggests that the evaluation aspect of public involvement could be given somewhat more attention. Lastly, the low level of participation in the project's open house event indicates that the general public was not a core stakeholder group. A similar observation has been reported for other open houses that are held in non-residential areas. But in this instance, it was reasonable to cover this angle just in case the public did have a general concern.

To sum up, the Goods Movement Strategy public-involvement effort was able to collect up-to-date information on truck movement patterns and their trends in Edmonton and created opportunities for industry participants to have a voice in the development of the Goods Movement Strategy. The project did not involve immediate changes to the urban landscape of Edmonton and did not immediately or directly affect the general public, and hence can be categorized as a nonsensitive project. Nevertheless, the raison d'etre for the City of Edmonton largely consists in its role as a transportation, industrial, and commercial hub for Northern Alberta and rural Western Canada. A well-planned and organized transportation system for goods movement is critical for Edmonton to fulfill this role; and, thus, this plan provides critical information and helps coordinate planning for future regional development.

Sources

1. Edmonton's Transportation Master Plan.
2. Goods Movement Strategy Public Involvement Plan, version 3.0.

3. Edmonton Goods Movement Strategy – Public and Stakeholder Consultation Final Report, January 2014.
4. The Way We Move 2013 Roadside Truck Survey Report.
5. www.edmonton.ca/city_government/city_vision_and_strategic_plan/goods-movement-strategy.aspx. (Accessed Oct. 1, 2016.)

CHAPTER 10

"The Way We Move" Transportation Master Plan

Early Engagement Effort

Heather Stewart and Paul R. Messinger

The Way We Move is the guiding document for Transportation planning and achieving the City strategic goal to "Shift Edmonton's Transportation Mode." This broader policy helps to provide context for specific transportation planning projects and their public-involvement plans (PIPs). However, "The Way We Move" was one of the earlier "Way" plans to be completed and its involvement activities were conducted before the Involving Edmonton public-involvement policy was fully implemented. Therefore it cannot itself be used as a template for high-level strategic planning public involvement, although extensive public involvement did take place.

Context and Catalyst

The "Way We Move" is the current 30-year Transportation Master Plan for Edmonton. It was released in June 2011 as an update to the previous 1999 Transportation Master Plan. It is one of six aligned strategic "Ways" plans in the City of Edmonton: Municipal Development (The Way We Grow), Environmental (The Way We Green), Health, Safety and Social Wellbeing (The Way We Live), Economic Growth and Diversification (The Way We Prosper), and Financial Sustainability (The Way We Finance). Each of these Strategic Plans reflects one of the six Strategic Goals of the City of Edmonton's 10-year "The Way Ahead" Strategic Plan toward the City Vision, which, in turn, aligns with the Province of Alberta's 2008 Capital Region Plan.

"The seven Transportation Strategic Goals are

- Transportation and Land Use Integration,
- Access and Mobility,
- Transportation Mode Shift.
- Sustainability,
- Health and Safety,
- Well-Maintained Infrastructure, and
- Economic Vitality"[1]

Planning and Engagement

"The Way We Move" is particularly aligned with "The Way We Grow" because transportation and municipal growth are so closely interconnected. In addition to alignment with other high-level Strategic Plans, The Way We Move was developed based on:

- "The comments, experiences and insights expressed by Edmontonians in public focus groups and stakeholder workshops;
- A review of best practices from other municipal jurisdictions; and
- An evaluation of best practices for use in the local context."[1]

The development of The Way We Move was initiated shortly after the creation of the Involving Edmonton public-involvement policy in 2006. Primary consultations for The Way We Move were conducted in early 2007 and reported on, in a 15-month update to council on public-involvement policy implementation in June 2007. Standard PIP templates were still under development at this time and were not created for these activities. However these consultations (public focus groups and stakeholder workshops) were considered early implementation outcomes of the Involving Edmonton policy.[2]

Impact on Subsequent Public Involvement and Decision-Making

The Way We Move creates guidelines that are balanced with future public involvement to inform Council and department planning decisions. Sometimes this is referenced directly in a PIP; for example, the Goods Movement Strategy PIP refers to it in the sections "Description Of The Overall Project Or Initiative," and in "The Scope (Impact, And Complexity) Of This Decision." The Scope section gives an indication of how the final strategy decision must align with The Way We Move: "The Goods Movement Strategy will follow the policy direction defined in *The Way We Move*, which is the overarching long-term plan guiding transportation decisions for the transportation system that is envisioned for 2040."[4] The West Rossdale Arterial Roadway Improvements PIP has a similar mention in Scope, while the 2013 Edmonton Bike Routes PIP references the Transportation Master Plan in the Decision-Maker section. A reference in Scope is the most common and seems to have evolved into the boiler-plate template for PIPs (see West and SE LRT Expansions PIP, 17th St. PIP, Mark Messier Trail PIP, 34th St PIP, 142nd St PIP, 105th Ave Corridor PIP, 112 Ave PIP, Whitemud Drive PIP, 149th Street Interchange at Yellowhead Trail PIP, Yellowhead Trail Corridor Stage 1 Implementation Plan PIP, 107 Avenue Corridor Improvements and Road Widening PIP, and the Guardian Road/Lewis Estates Boulevard Widening PIP.)[5]

Other PIPs do not directly reference The Way We Move; for example, The North-West LRT PIP from 2010 does not mention The Way We

Move Transportation Master Plan at all, although decisions would still have been made in reference to that plan. This may be an artifact of earlier PIP processes before the now-ubiquitous text was adopted as the de-facto template within Scope, especially since a 2012 PIP for subsequent North-West LRT public involvement does include the standard Scope reference to The Way We Move. The PIP for Arterial Roadway Widening Projects: 34 Street—23 to 34 Avenue & 23 Avenue do not reference The Way We Move but do reference subplans that are themselves aligned with The Way We Move (Design and Construction Standards, Arterial Widening Program, Urban Traffic Noise Policy). Similarly, the 102 Avenue over Groat Road Bridge Replacement PIP does not reference the Way We Move. These examples are exceptions to the general rule.[5]

Assessment and Learning

Each of the seven Transportation Strategic Goals are monitored and evaluated for progress, and a 54-page Progress Measures Report was issued in June 2012. Interestingly, the terms "public involvement," "engagement," or "consultation" were not used in the Project Measures report.[6] Nevertheless, the references to The Way We Move in the vast majority of PIPs indicate that there is an impact. However, there could be greater consistency in the level of detail and the PIP section used for referencing guiding plans and policies (the frontrunner being Scope).

The 2011 Transportation Services' Current Public Involvement Practices Report to Council explains that "the Transportation Master Plan, *The Way We Move*, is a high-level strategic plan. Public involvement for this and other major strategic planning activities would involve a wide range of stakeholders and likely include all geographic areas of the city with the outcome reflecting citizen values related to transportation and set general direction for the future."[7,6] It is unfortunate that the full PIP process was not in place at the time of The Way We Move's public-involvement activities in 2007, since that makes it more difficult to assess the extent to which that goal was achieved. There are no references to public-involvement activities subsequent to 2007, although the final plan report was not released until 2011.

Overall, The Way We Move provides a framework that helps to set goals and build consistency in Transportation planning. There is emerging consistency in the use of The Way We Move in PIPs to help situate specific planning projects in the broader context, though there are exceptions. Unfortunately The Way We Move itself cannot be used as a model for public involvement because its involvement activities were conducted before the Involving Edmonton policy was fully implemented.

Sources

1. City of Edmonton, The Way We Move: Transportation Master Plan (September 2009) http://www.edmonton.ca/city_government/city_vision_and_strategic_plan/the-way-we-move.aspx (accessed October 1, 2016).

2. City of Edmonton, Implementation of City Policy C513-City of Edmonton Public.

3. Involvement Policy – Update (June 2007); http://www.edmonton.ca/for_residents/C513.pdf (accessed October 1, 2016).

4. City of Edmonton, Goods Movement Strategy Public Involvement Plan Version 3, (2012).

5. All Other PIPs.

6. City of Edmonton, The Way We Move Progress Measures, June 2011.

7. City of Edmonton, Transportation Services' Current Public Involvement Practices Report to Council, June 2011.

References

Suggested Readings

Readings on Public Involvement (* highly cited[1], ** very highly cited[2])

Abelson, J., Forest, P., Eyles, J., Smith, P., Martin, E., and Gauvin, F. (2003). Deliberations about deliberative methods: Issues in the design and evaluation of public participation processes. *Social Science and Medicine*, 57, 239–251.**

Adria, M., and Mao, Y. (2011). Chapter 35: Encouraging public involvement in public policymaking through university-government collaboration, in *Higher Education, Emerging Technologies, and Community Partnerships: Concepts, Models and Practices*, eds., Boyden, M. and Carpenter, R., 374–380.

Beierle, T., and Konisky, D. (2000). Values, conflict, and trust in participatory environmental planning. *Journal of Policy Analysis and Management*, 19(4), 587–602.*

Bickerstaff, K., Tolley, R., and Walker, G. (2002). Transport planning and participation: The rhetoric and realities of public involvement. *Journal of Transport Geography*, 10, 61–73.*

Boxelaar, L., Paine, M., and Beilin, R. (2006). Community engagement and public administration: Of silos, overlays and technologies of government. *Australian Journal of Public Administration*, 65(1), 113–126.

Bryson, J. M., Quick, K. S., Slotterback, C. S., Crosby, B. C. (2012). Designing public participation processes. In *Public Administration Review*, ed., Moynihan, D. P. 73(1), 23–34.*

Chilvers, J. (2008). Deliberating competence: Theoretical and practitioner perspectives on effective participatory appraisal practice. *Science, Technology and Human Values*, 33(2), 155–185.*

Denhardt, J., and Campbell, K. (2006). The role of democratic values in transformational leadership. *Administration and Society*, 38(5), 556–572.

Christensen, C. M. (1997). *The Innovator's Dilemma: When New Technologies Cause Great Firms to Fail*, Boston, MA: Harvard Business School Press.**

Grunig, J. E. (Ed.) (1992). *Excellence in public relations and communication management*, Hillsdale, NJ: Lawrence Erlbaum Associates (reprinted by Routledge in 2008).**

---

[1] Between 100 and 500 citations as of July 2016.

[2] More than 500 citations as of July 2016.

Hardiker, N. R. and Grant, M. J. (2011). Factors that influence public engagement with eHealth: A literature review. *International Journal of Medical Informatics*, 80(1), 1–12.

Henriks, C. (2006). When the forum meets interest politics: Strategic uses of public deliberation. *Politics and Society*, 34(4), 571-602.*

Höppner, C., Frick, J., and Buchecker, M. (2007). Assessing psycho-social effects of participatory landscape planning. *Landscape and Urban planning*, 83(2), 196–207.

Kathlene, L. and Martin, J. A. (1991). Enhancing citizen participation: Panel designs, perspectives, and policy formation. *Journal of Policy Analysis and Management*, 1011, 46–63.*

Mao, Y., and Adria, M. (2013). Deciding who will decide: Assessing random selection for participants in Edmonton's Citizen Panel on budget priorities. *Canadian Public Administration/Administration publique du Canada*, 56(4), 607–34.

Michels, A., and De Graaf, L. (2010). Examining citizen participation: Local participatory policy making and democracy. *Local Government Studies*, 36(4), 477–491.*

Nabatchi, T. (2010). Addressing the citizenship and democratic deficits: The potential of deliberative democracy for public administration. *The American Review of Public Administration*, 40(4) 376–399.*

Rowe, G. and Frewer, L. J. (2000). Public participation methods: A framework for evaluation. *Science, Technology and Human Values*, 25(1), 3–29.**

Rowe, G. and Frewer, L. J. (2004). Evaluating public-participation exercises: A research agenda. *Science, Technology and Human Values*, 29(4), 512–556.**

Rowe, G. and Frewer, L. J. (2005). A typology of public engagement mechanisms. *Science, Technology and Human Values*, 30(2), 251–290.**

Rowe, G., Horlick-Jones, T., Walls, J., and Pidgeon, N. (2005). Difficulties in evaluating public engagement initiatives: Reflections on an evaluation of the UK GM Nation? Public debate about transgenic crops. *Public Understanding of Science*, 14(4), 331–352.*

Rowe, G., Horlick-Jones, T., Walls, J., Poortinga, W., and Pidgeon, N. F. (2008). Analysis of a normative framework for evaluating public engagement exercises: Reliability, validity and limitations. *Public Understanding of Science*, 17(4), 419–441.

Ryzin, G. G., Muzzio, D., Immerwahr, S., Gulick, L., and Martinez, E. (2004). Drivers and consequences of citizen satisfaction: An application of the American customer satisfaction index model to New York City. *Public Administration Review*, 64(3), 331–341.*

White, S. S. (2001). Public participation and organizational change in Wisconsin land use management. *Land Use Policy*, 18, 341–350.

Yang, K. (2003). Neoinstitutionalism and E-Government: Beyond Jane Fountain. *Social Science Computer Review*, 21(4), 432–442.

Readings on e-Government and Participatory Government

Batley, R. (1996). Public–private relationships and performance in service provision. *Urban Studies*, 33(4-5), 723–751.*

Bovaird, T. (2004). Public–private partnerships: From contested concepts to prevalent practice. *International Review of Administrative Sciences*, 70(2), 199–215.*

Bonsón, E, Torres, L., Royo, S., and Flores, F. (2012). Local e-government 2.0: Social media and corporate transparency in municipalities. *Government Information Quarterly*, 29(2), 123–132.*

Ciupuliga, A. R., and Cuppen, E. (2013). The role of dialogue in fostering acceptance of transmission lines: The case of a France-Spain interconnection project. *Energy Policy*, 60, 224–233.

Entwistle, T., and Martin, S. (2005). From competition to collaboration in public service delivery: A new agenda for research, *Public Administration*, 83(1), 233–242.*

Hart, O. (2003). Incomplete contracts and public ownership: Remarks, and an application to public–private partnerships. *The Economic Journal*, 113 (March), C69–C76.**

Kaplan, A. M., and Haenlein, M. (2010). Users of the World, Unite! The challenges and opportunities of social media. *Business Horizons*, 53, 59–68.**

Mossberger, K., Wu, Y., and Crawford, J. (2013). Connecting citizens and local governments? Social media and interactivity in major US cities. *Government Information Quarterly*, 30(4) 351–358.

Sjoberg, G. (1960). *The Preindustrial City, Past and Present*. Glenco, IL: Free Press.*

Tiebout, C. (1956). A pure theory of local expenditures. *Journal of Political Economy*, 64(5), 416–424.**

Wang, X., and Bryer, T. (2012). Assessing the costs of public participation: A case study of two online participation mechanisms. *American Review of Public Administration*, 43(2), 179–199.

Background References on Service, e-Service, Self-service, and Disruptive Technologies

Alam, I. (2002). An exploratory investigation of user involvement in new service development. *Journal of the Academy of Marketing Science*, 30, 250–261.**

Bateson, J. E. (1985). Self-service consumer: An exploratory study. *Journal of Retailing*, 61(3), 49–76.**

Bitner, M. J. (1992). Servicescapes: The impact of physical surroundings on customers and employees. *Journal of Marketing*, 56, 57–71.**

Bitner, M. J., Booms, B. H., and Tetreault, M. S. (1990). The service encounter: Diagnosing favorable and unfavorable incidents. *Journal of Marketing*, 54, 71–84.**

Bitner, M. J., Brown, S. W. and Meuter M. L. (2000). Technology infusion in service encounters. *Journal of the Academy of Marketing Science*, 28(1), 138–149.**

Bitner, M. J., Ostrom, A., and Meuter, M. L. (2002). Implementing successful self-service technologies. *Academy of Management Executive*, 16(4), 96–109.*

Bower, J. L. and Christensen, C. M. (1995). Disruptive Technologies: Catching the Wave Harvard Business Review, January–February 1995. hbr.org/1995/01/disruptive-technologies-catching-the-wave. **

Brown, S., and Swartz, T. (1989). A gap analysis of professional service quality. *Journal of Marketing*, 53(2), 92–98.**

Carman, J. (1990). Consumer perceptions of service quality – An assessment of the SERVQUAL dimensions. *Journal of Marketing*, 66(1), 33–55.**

Christensen, C. M. (1997). *The Innovator's Dilemma: When New Technologies Cause Great Firms to Fail*, Boston, MA: Harvard Business School Press.**

Cronin, J., and Taylor, S. (1992). Measuring service quality – A reexamination and extension. *Journal of Marketing*, 56(3), 55–68.**

Cronin, J., and Taylor, S. (1994). SERVPERF Versus SERVQUAL-reconciling performance-based and perceptions-minus-expectations measurement of service quality. *Journal of Marketing*, 58(1), 125–131.**

Curran, J. M. and Meuter, M. L. (2005). Self-service technology adoption: Comparing three technologies. *Journal of Services Marketing*, 19(2), 103–113.*

Curran, J. M., Meuter, M. L., and Surprenant, C. F. (2003). Intentions to use self-service Technologies: A confluence of multiple attitudes. *Journal of Service Research*, 5(3), 209–224.*

Dabholkar, P. A. (1996). Consumer evaluations of new technology-based self-service options: An investigation of alternative models of service quality. *International Journal of Research in Marketing*, 13(1), 29–51.*

Dabholkar, P. A., and Bagozzi, R. P. (2002). An attitudinal model of technology-based self-service: Moderating effects of consumer traits and situational factors. *Journal of the Academy of Marketing Science*, 30(3), 184–101.**

Deacon, R. T. and Sonstelie, J. (1985). Rationing by waiting and the value of time: Results from a natural experiment, *Journal of Political Economy*, 93, 627–647.

Etgar, M. (2008). A descriptive model of the consumer co-production process. *Journal of the Academy of Marketing Science*, 36(1), 97–108.**

Fisk, R. P., and Brown, S. W. (1993). Tracking the evolution of the services marketing literature. *Journal of Retailing*, 69(1), 61–103.**

Fitzsimmons, J. A. (2003). Is self-service the future of services? *Managing Service Quality*, 13(6), 443–444.

Hartline, M. D., and Ferrell, O. C. (1996). The management of customer-contact service employees: An empirical investigation. *Journal of Marketing*, 60(4), 52–70.**

Hogan, J., Hogan, R, and Busch, C. M. (1984). How to measure service orientation. *Journal of Applied Psychology*, 69(1), 167–173.**

Hollins, G., and Hollins, W. (2002). *Total Design. Managing the Design Process in the Service Sector*. London: Trans Atlantic Publications. (Original work published in 1991).*

Hui, M. K. and Bateson, J. E. G. (1991). Perceived control and the effects of crowding and consumer choice on the service experience. *Journal of Consumer Research*, 18(2) (Sep.), 174–184.**

Jiang, J., Klein, G., and Carr, C. (2002). Measuring information system service quality: SERVQUAL from the other side. *MIS Quarterly*, 26(2), 145–166.**

Joseph, M., McClure, C., and Joseph, B. (1999). Service quality in the banking sector: The impact of technology on service delivery. *International Journal of Bank Marketing*, 17(4), 182–191.*

Kettinger, W., and Lee, C. (2005). Zones of tolerance: Alternative scales for measuring information systems service quality. *MIS Quarterly*, 29(4), 607–623.*

Lee, J., and Allaway, A. (2002). Effects of personal control on adoption of self-service technology innovations. *The Journal of Services Marketing*, 16(6), 553–572.*

Lovelock, C. H. (1983). Classifying services to gain strategic marketing insights. *Journal of Marketing*, 47(3), 9–20.**

Lovelock, C. H., and Wirtz, J. (2007). *Service Marketing: People, Technology, Strategy* (6th edition). Upper Saddle River, New Jersey: Pearson Prentice Hall.**

Lytle, R., Hom, P. W., and Mokwa, M. P. (1998). SERV*OR: A managerial measure of organizational service-orientation. *Journal of Marketing*, 74(4), 455–489.*

Maglio, P. P., Srinivasan, S., Kreulen, J. T., and Spohrer, J. (2006). Service systems, service scientists, SSME, and innovation. *Communications of the ACM*, 49(7) (July), 81–85.**

Maglio, P. P., and Spohrer, J. (2008). Fundamentals of service science. *Journal of the Academy of Marketing Science*, 36, 18–20.**

Messinger, P. R. (2013). Municipal service delivery: A multi-stakeholder framework, *Human Factors and Ergonomics in Manufacturing and Service Industries*, 23(1), 37–46.

Messinger, P. R., Li, J., Stroulia, E., Galletta, D., Ge, X., and Choi, S. (2009). Seven challenges to combining human and automated service. *Canadian Journal of Administrative Sciences*, 26, 267–285.

Meuter, M. L., Bitner, M. J., Ostrom, A. L., and Brown, S. W. (2005). Choosing among alternative service delivery modes: An investigation of customer trial of self-service technologies. *Journal of Marketing*, 69(2) (Apr.), 61–83.**

Meuter, M. L., Ostrom, A. L, Roundtree, R. I., and Bitner, M.J. (2000). Self-service technologies: Understanding customer satisfaction with technology-based service encounters. *Journal of Marketing*, 64(3), 50–64.**

Normann, R. and Ramirez, R. (1993). From value chain to value constellation: Designing interactive strategy. *Harvard Business Review*, 71 (July–August), 65–77.**

Parasuraman A., Zeithaml V., and Berry, L. (1985). A conceptual model of service quality and its implications for future research. *Journal of Marketing*, 49(4), 41–50.**

Parasuraman, A, Zeithaml, V., and Berry, L. (1988). SERVQUAL – A multiple-item scale for measuring consumer perceptions of service quality. *Journal of Retailing*, 64(1), 12–40.**

Parasuraman, A., Zeithaml, V., and Berry, L. (1994). Alternative scales for measuring service quality – A comparative-assessment based on psychometric and diagnostic criteria. *Journal of Retailing*, 70(3), 201–230.**

Parasuraman, A., Zeithaml, V., and Malhotra, A. (2005). E-S-QUAL – A multiple-item scale for assessing electronic service quality. *Journal of Service Research*, 7(3), 213–233.**

Pitt, L., Watson, R., and Kavan, C. (1995). Service quality: A measure of information-systems effectiveness. *MIS Quarterly*, 19(2), 173–187.**

Reitman, D. (1991). Endogenous quality differentiation in congested markets, *The Journal of Industrial Economics*, 39(6) (Dec.), 621–647.

Saxe, R., and Weitz, B. A. (1982). The SOCO scale: A measure of the customer orientation of salespeople. *Journal of Marketing Research*, 19(3) (Aug), 343–351.**

Schumpeter, J. A. (2014) [1942]. *Capitalism, Socialism and Democracy* (2nd edition). Floyd, Virginia: Impact Books.**

Shostack, G. L. (1977). Breaking free from product marketing. *Journal of Marketing*, 41(Summer), 73–80.**

Shostack, G. L. (1987). Service positioning through structural change. *Journal of Marketing*, 59(January), 34–43.**

Shostack, G. L. (2001). How to design a service. *European Journal of Marketing*, 16(1), 49–63.**

Solomon, M. R., Surprenant, C., Czepiel, J. A., and Gutman, E. G. (1985). A role theory perspective on dyadic interactions: The service encounter. *Journal of Marketing*, 49(1), 99–111.**

Spohrer, J., Maglio, P. P., Bailey, J., and Gruhl, D. (2007). Steps toward a science of service systems. *Computer*, 40(1) (Jan.), 71–77.**

Teas, R. (1994). Expectations as a comparison standard in measuring service quality – An assessment of a reassessment. *Journal of Marketing*, 58(1), 132–139.*

Van Dyke, T. P., Kappelman, L. A., and Prybutok, V. R. (1997). Measuring information systems service quality: Concerns on the use of the SERVQUAL questionnaire. *MIS Quarterly*, 21(2), 195–208.**

Vargo, S. L., and Lusch, R. F. (2004). Evolving to a new dominant logic for marketing. *Journal of Marketing*, 68(1), 1–17.**

Vargo, S. L. and Lusch, R. F.(2008). Service-dominant logic: Continuing the evolution. *Journal of the Academy of Marketing Science*, 36(1), 1–10.**

Wang, Y., Wang, Y., Lin, H., and Tang, T. (2003). Determinants of user acceptance of internet banking: An empirical study. *International Journal of Service Industry Management*, 14(5), 501–519.**

Woo, K., and Ennew, C. (2005). Measuring business-to-business professional service quality and its consequences. *Journal of Business Research*, 58(9), 1178–1185.*

Xie, C., Bagozzi, R. P., Troye, S. V. (2008). Trying to prosume: Toward a theory of consumers as co-creators of value, *Journal of the Academy of Marketing Science*, 36(1), 109–122.*

Zeithaml, V., Bitner, M. J., and Gremler, D. (2006). *Services Marketing: Integrating Customer Focus Across the Firm* (4th edition). Boston, MA: McGraw-Hill, pp. 267–276.**

Zeithaml, V., Parasuraman, A., and Berry, L. (1985). Problems and strategies in service marketing. *Journal of Marketing*, 49 (Spring), 33–46.**

List of Contributors

Dr. Marco Adria is Professor Emeritus of Communication at the University of Alberta and founder of the Centre for Public Involvement, a research and development institute operated by the University of Alberta and the City of Edmonton. He is coeditor of *Handbook of research in citizen engagement and public participation in the era of new media* (IGI Global, 2016). He was a visiting professor in the Department of Business at the Tecnológico de Monterrey, Mexico, in 2015 to 2016. His book, *Technology and Nationalism* (Montreal: McGill-Queen's University Press, 2010) won the Lewis Mumford Award for Outstanding Scholarship in the Ecology of Technics, awarded by the New York based Media Ecology Association.

E. C. LeSage is professor emeritus in the Faculty of Extension at the University of Alberta. Over a 32-year academic career, his research, teaching, and scholarship foci addressed provincial and municipal institutional and administrative reform, the practice of university continuing education, public administration professionalism, and engaged citizenry. He provided academic leadership for governmental studies programs at the Faculty of Extension and served as associate dean (academic) under two deans. He holds a PhD in political science (Carleton University) and lives in retirement on Vancouver Island.

Fiona Cavanagh is Director of Consultation for the Government of Alberta, Executive Council, Public Affairs Bureau. Fiona served for five years as inaugural Executive Director of the Centre for Public Involvement, a partnership between the University of Alberta and the City of Edmonton to advance research and practice of public engagement. She has extensive expertise in design, evaluation, and community-based research of public engagement. She was Program Manager of Public Engagement for Change for Children. She served twice as chair of the International Association of Public Participation (IAP2) North

American Conferences on Public Participation and is on the City of Edmonton Mayor's Task Force to End Poverty. She holds an MEd in Educational Policy Studies from the University of Alberta and a certificate in Public Participation from IAP2. In 2014, Fiona was named one of Edmonton's Top Women in Business by, Edmonton online magazine, the Wanderer.

Moein Khanlari is an Assistant Professor of marketing at the University of New Hampshire where he teaches courses on consumer analytics and conducts research on services and consumer decision making. Moein holds a PhD in Marketing from the University of Alberta and his doctoral research on extended service contracts was a finalist for the 2015 IBM Service Science Best Student Paper Award by the Institute for Operations Research and the Management Sciences (INFORMS). His interest in understanding how public and private organizations can deliver outstanding services to their constituents and customers finds clear expression in the current work on public engagement in governmental service delivery.

Rosslynn Zulla is a PhD candidate in the School of Public Health at the University of Alberta in Edmonton, Alberta, Canada. She has worked on grant-writing, research and community development projects in community, hospital, and university settings as an analyst, coordinator, grant-writer and junior investigator. Her research experience includes health promotion, medical education, research methods (particularly from a participatory worldview), developmental disabilities, settlement studies, and mental health. She has taught undergraduate and graduate research methods at the University of Calgary, Faculty of Social Work. Presently, she is conducting related research in universities (e.g., University of Calgary and University of Alberta) and national research institutes (e.g., NeuroDevNet).

Heather Stewart has worked with the Canadian Network of Women's Shelters and Transition Houses for two years as the Knowledge Management and Creation Project Officer. She has a Master of Arts in Political Science from the University of Alberta focusing on the role of not-for-profit organizations as advocates and knowledge brokers for policy discourse between communities and government and has worked with organizations such as the Centre for Public Involvement, Cuso International, and the Community Foundation of Ottawa. Her projects with the Network include the Practice Exchange, Open Doors Inclusive Service Model Regional Support Networks, and Communities of Practice with the Shelters of the Future.

Michelle Chalifoux is Public Engagement Program Manager at City of Edmonton. She previously served as Communications Specialist, Communications and External Relations, Grant MacEwan University, and Public Affairs Officer, Government of Alberta. She holds a BA in Political Science from the University of Alberta and a Diploma in Public Relations from Grant Macewan University. She has extensive experience with stakeholder and community engagement, communications strategy and planning, community development, government, media relations, and internal communications.

Index

OTHER TITLES IN OUR SERVICE SYSTEMS AND INNOVATIONS IN BUSINESS AND SOCIETY COLLECTION

Jim Spohrer, IBM and Haluk Demirkan, Arizona State University, Editors

- *Modeling Service Systems* by Ralph Badinelli
- *Sustainable Service* by Adi Wolfson
- *Fair Pay: Adaptively Win-Win Customer Relationships* by Richard Reisman
- *Business Engineering and Service Design, Second Edition* by Oscar Barros
- *Service Design with Applications to Health Care Institutions* by Oscar Barros
- *Obtaining Value from Big Data for Service Delivery* by Stephen H. Kaisler, Frank Armour, and William Money
- *Service Innovation* by Anders Gustafsson, Per Kristensson, Gary R. Schirr, and Lars Witell
- *Matching Services to Markets: The Role of the Human Sensorium in Shaping Service-Intensive Markets* by H.B. Casanova
- *Achieving Success through Innovation: Cases and Insights from the Hospitality, Travel, and Tourism Industry* by Glenn Withiam
- *Designing Service Processes to Unlock Value, Second Edition* by Joy M. Field

Announcing the Business Expert Press Digital Library

Concise e-books business students need for classroom and research

This book can also be purchased in an e-book collection by your library as

- a one-time purchase,
- that is owned forever,
- allows for simultaneous readers,
- has no restrictions on printing, and
- can be downloaded as PDFs from within the library community.

Our digital library collections are a great solution to beat the rising cost of textbooks. E-books can be loaded into their course management systems or onto students' e-book readers. The **Business Expert Press** digital libraries are very affordable, with no obligation to buy in future years. For more information, please visit **www.businessexpertpress.com/librarians**. To set up a trial in the United States, please email **sales@businessexpertpress.com**.

CPSIA information can be obtained
at www.ICGtesting.com
Printed in the USA
FSHW021651021219
64505FS